# A Prairie Town Goes to War

Jenni Mortin

*For dear Maria
a new friend
Jenni Mortin*

**National Library of Canada Cataloguing in Publication Data**

Mortin, Jenni, 1940-
   A Prairie town goes to war / Jenni Mortin.
     Includes bibliographical references and index.

   ISBN 1-55246-538-1

1. World War, 1939-1945--Personal narratives, Canadian.
2. Soldiers--Saskatchewan--Dilke--Correspondence.  3. Dilke (Sask.)--
Biography.  I. Title.

D811.A2M66 2003        940.54'8171        C2003-906619-3

*Printed in Canada*
*First Printing, November 2003*

*All Inquiries and Orders:*
George A. Vanderburgh, *Publisher*
THE BATTERED SILICON DISPATCH BOX™
*e-Mail:* gav@bmts.com  *  *Fax:* (519) 925-3482

P. O. Box 204
Shelburne, Ontario
CANADA L0N 1S0

P. O. Box 122
Sauk City, Wisconsin
U.S.A. 53583-0122

This book is dedicated
to the people of Dilke
who served their country during
the Second World War,
and to those at home
who supported them through
the Dilke Active Service Comfort Club

# CONTENTS

Belgium
Oct. 3, '44.

Dear Mrs Martin and friends,

Well here I am again thanking you so much for what I call well appreciated cigarettes. Really do not know what _____ would do for smokes if it was not for you folks. Well we are driving on as usual old Jerry just does not seem to be able to hold the Canadians back, when the boys get mad, Jerry pulls out. We went to take Dieppe, but when we got there no Germans, they knew we were out for avenge and pulled out rather than face us. Canada has a wonderfull name in France, and we have adopted Caen as that was where Hitler lost the war, he really took a beating there, we had our share of it too, but he got the worst end. The wife is fine she says she has a lovely home ready for me for when I get back, so you

Fred Blancheon of the South Saskatchewan Regiment just casually mentioned his return visit to Dieppe early in September 1944.

# A Prairie Town
# Goes to War

## Foreword

WHILE helping my parents move out of their long-time home in 1999, I came across the Second World War letters which inspired this book about the overseas service of the men and women of Dilke, Saskatchewan — my hometown — and the sturdy little organization that supported them. My mother, Helen Mortin, was the third and final secretary of the Dilke Active Service Comfort Club, which sent letters and parcels, cigarettes, chocolates and chewing gum to the Dilke people who served Canada abroad from 1940 through 1946. When the Club faded away with the war, she packed the letters it received from abroad with the minutes and other documents into a small box which was then forgotten for half a century. When I stumbled upon this treasure trove, many of the letters looked little older than the day they were mailed. The flaps of some were stuck down so it seemed they had never been opened.

After reading the letters, I was compelled to seek out the survivors among their authors and talk to them about their war experiences and their memories of the Comfort Club. Lamentably few are left. They live in the Dilke area, in other parts of Saskatchewan, in Alberta and northern British Columbia. Some I had known throughout my childhood; others I had never met. Talking with them was a joy. All remember Dilke and its well-named Comfort Club with great fondness, and they put a hometown face on the familiar war story.

I hope this book comes close to representing their wartime experiences and adventures, and I dedicate it to them and all the others from our little town who were prepared to serve wherever Canada needed them. And to the Comfort Club which supported them so strongly throughout the war, to my mother and its other indefatigable secretaries, and to my father, Ernie Mortin, on whose memory I so often relied as I wrote. Any errors, of course, are mine. The letters and other Club materials are earmarked for the Saskatchewan Archives in Regina.

*Harold Buck wrote 14 times to the Comfort Club during more than three years overseas.*

# I.

# "WE ARE NOT SO FAR AWAY AFTER ALL"

THERE was this little prairie town, and its name was Dilke. Just a wide place, really, in the road between the wheatfields, a tiny Saskatchewan village with 107 residents in 1941. Another 468 lived on the farms that stretched to the horizon in every direction, farms only beginning to recover from the drought, wind and grasshoppers that all but destroyed them and the province during the Dirty Thirties. Dilke people had endured 1937, the worst year in Saskatchewan's history when net farm income totalled $-36.3 million, and 1938 and 1939, somewhat better. In 1940, something that could be called a real crop was harvested and net farm income jumped to $96 million, but now Canada was at war and some of the men who would have helped in that long-awaited harvest had gone to learn more martial skills. First a trickle and then a flood of Dilke's young men and women went off to the Second World War to fight for freedom and democracy, 101 in all. Some of them had left home during the Depression years to find work elsewhere, but they remained Dilke's children.

There was this little prairie town and its name — in England, Italy, France, Germany and everywhere war tossed its sons and daughters — was love. Love was fitted in around the cookies, shaving cream, knitted socks, tomato juice and other items in the parcels the Dilke Active Service Comfort Club sent to its children overseas from October of 1940 to long past V-E Day. Love travelled with the cigarettes,

9

chocolates and chewing gum that pursued those children to the steep mountains and flooded rivers of Italy and to North Africa's broiling sands, to busy aircrews and army training schemes in Britain, and finally through the deadly months of slogging battle across France, Belgium and Holland to Germany.

This is the story of the 62 men and women of Dilke who served overseas during the Second World War, and of the Comfort Club created by their friends, neighbours and families to support them. It's based on hundreds of letters and cards of thanks sent to the Club from 1940 to 1946 and treasured still by its final secretary; on interviews with many of the men who returned from overseas and were still active as the century turned, and with the families of others; and on the minutes and accounts of the small but mighty organization that involved an entire community. It's a story of sacrifice and love, of adventure, adversity and triumph, a tiny microcosm of Canada's tremendous war effort.

*     *     *

More than an ocean separated the people of Dilke, sheltered in the familiar and safe, from the experiences of their young men and women in Canada's fighting forces. Even had the censors permitted, how could pilot Sam Side have explained in a letter about the 'gardening' he and his RCAF bomber crew did night after night over Europe? How could Fred Blancheon have relayed to folks at home the bitter, bloody schmozzle at Dieppe that smashed the South Saskatchewan Regiment? Whitney Barry and Lloyd Carr, Charlie Reid and Clarence Wray wrote from slit trenches and tents in the wintry mountains of Italy, but glossed over the deadly reality of day after demanding day of combat. Charlie Ell only once referred to the Forces dance band in which he played saxophone, and which provided such pleasure to Canadians in Britain. His brother Joe did not mention the day King George VI pinned Distinguished Flying Crosses on him, his pilot and navigator during an all-Canadian investiture at Buckingham Palace. And who at home would have understood Lloyd Smith's disgust that after three years of training, a German shell took him out of action after less than a month and a half in France? Today we can learn about all of these.

The reality of war walled Dilke off from its people overseas, but some things made it over that wall. Farming, of course, for these farmers' sons; their letters are full of references to the crops at home. "I am very pleased to hear that you have a great crop this year," Flying Officer Tom Koch wrote from RCAF 401 Squadron on November 9, 1942. "For years I hoped to see that, and now that we have it, I am not there. I am not sorry, but only regret that I cannot help you harvest it." He was flying one of the squadron's new Spitfires against German fighters over Britain and the Channel, but still thrilled that "we" had harvested part of the biggest wheat crop Saskatchewan had yet seen. Without the varying demands of the farming year, artilleryman Harold Buck found it difficult to remember what month it was. "Time goes by over here without much change in events," he wrote. "Not like home where you know that April and May are seeding time, wheat in head tells you it is July and when you start thinking about cutting it is usually the last part of August — and so on for every month of the year."

Far from the fields they knew, they examined other farms and crops. Art Boehme, part of the ground crew of RCAF 419 Squadron, wrote in 1942 that frost on June 11 spoiled some English crops. No doubt reflecting recent Saskatchewan experience, he added, "For all that it still looks like a bumper crop to me, but the farmers here don't think so." The following year he reported that England was likely to have its largest crop ever. "Thousands of acres have been broken up since the war and if they keep all this land under cultivation after the war, Western Canada will have to, to a certain extent, resort to other means of making a living." Every English farm had to have half its land under cultivation, he said, whereas before the war some farmers with 200 acres had plowed up only 10 acres.

English farmers welcomed harvest help, so these Canadians could get a close-up of how things were done. They were not always impressed. "For the past month in the evenings and on my days off I have been going stooking and stacking sheaves for the farmers at two shillings an hour," Reece Jones of RCAF 431 Squadron wrote on September 14, 1943. "I like the work and the farmers are pleased to get some help with the harvest ... The farmers in this country are about fifty years behind the times in farming. They still use the two-wheeled cart and one horse to haul sheaves and the old threshing machines that you cut the twine with a knife and feed the sheaves by hand." The men of 419 Squadron were too busy to work in the fields that fall, Art Boehme said. "Anyway I don't believe any of us could do a good day's physical labour now." A year later he proved himself wrong, spending a seven-day leave on a farm in Suffolk, where he drove a tractor for three days to cut the grain.

Three weeks after he landed in France on D-Day with the artillery's 13th Field Regiment, Stuart Laing wrote that the countryside reminded him of home. "The wheat and oats are about three to four feet high (That ain't Saskatchewan, did I hear somebody say?) and all in head. It sort of makes one feel at home to wade through it. Some fields are taking quite a beating though." In Germany with the Occupation Force a year later, Gunnar Gustafson was struck by the differences with Canadian farms. "First, in the majority of cases you will find their house and barn all built together in one large building. Everything is on a smaller scale. Maybe ten to twenty hens, a few cows and usually a goat and the odd place a handful of sheep. In the gardens corn, beets, radish, tomatoes and vines are very seldom seen.... Women are expected to work in the fields all day the same as the men, but have to give them credit for they are really a hard working race."

\*       \*       \*

Wherever they went, the Comfort Club parcels found them. In November 1942, Tom Koch described the joy those parcels brought. "One cannot help but feel lonely at times, wishing he were back at home among the people he grew up with and seeing friendly faces around ... A parcel like this brings a bit of Dilke to me ... I am proud to be one of the many boys from Dilke over here, representing our tiny village and trying to put it on the map with large letters." That was just one of the parcels he and the other 61 Dilke people who served overseas received from the Comfort Club. At least four boxes a year went off to each of them, containing a dozen or more items more valuable than gold to people living and often fighting in a foreign land. At the heart of each was a package of precious cookies baked with real butter and sugar in the kitchens of home, and nothing could have brought that home closer.

From every arena of war, they sent back their heartfelt thanks, as much for the remembering and the letters filled with home news as for the cookies and tomato juice, canned meat, knitted socks, razor blades or toothpaste. "A parcel from home makes us feel you haven't forgotten us over here," Trooper Steve Eberts of 4th Reconnaissance Regiment (Princess Louise Dragoon Guards) wrote from Italy on January 28, 1944. Sam Side of RCAF heavy bomber 428 Squadron based at Middleton St. George in County Durham was inspired to poetry that May:

> Oh, it isn't so much the chocolate bar,
> Or the package of chewing gum;
> It isn't the smokes or the book of jokes
> That cheer when you're feeling glum;
> It isn't the can of pork & beans
> Though the taste is certainly grand,
> Or milk or Spam, though they seem to a man
> Like a bit of Canada canned.
>
> No, these are not the important things
> In a parcel that comes from home,
> That isn't the part that cheers the heart
> Of a man when he's all alone;
> When you come to camp and a parcel's there
> From the folks far over the sea,
> The feeling that stays thru the endless days
> Is, someone remembers me.
>
> Oh, a parcel from home just hits the spot
> In a way you will never know;
> We fully appreciate that you work till late,
> Filling parcels all in a row
> With the food & necessities that we require.

On behalf of the Dilke boys in the ranks,
To all the members for the kind deeds rendered,
Please accept our heartiest thanks.

The Dilke Active Service Comfort Club sent at least 526 parcels to people of the district serving overseas (the minutes and accounts are not always precise and peter out in early 1946, though thanks were received in May that year from a man still in Germany with the Occupation Force). Directly from the manufacturers went much-wanted Canadian cigarettes and boxes of chocolates or chewing gum. Even today, the 331 letters on thin airmail paper and the 143 cards of thanks are redolent of homesickness and adventure in a foreign world, determination to do the job and eagerness to get back to "real" life.

The women who packed the parcels chose the contents well. They sent "things which are hard to get over here, especially canned meat, and which are most appreciated," Art Boehme wrote on June 6, 1943. Just five months after he arrived in England, 20-year-old Trooper Butch Side of A Squadron, Canadian Armoured Corps Reinforcement Unit, told the Comfort Club that his parcel contained "everything a soldier, or should say serviceman, requires, for instance laundry soap, and by the way when I return I'll give you ladies a demonstration on how to wash clothes (I don't mind the washing part of it but what hurts is having to wear them afterwards.)"

The cookies were especially welcome. "Let's hope that every cookie means a bullet for Hitler and his mob," Clarence Wray said militantly on June 4, 1942; a year later, he would be firing artillery shells in Sicily. When Leo Selinger of the Queen's Own Cameron Highlanders of Canada saw the cookies in the parcel he received on February 3, 1944, "I felt like sitting down and eating until I was blue in the face but when the boys come around and helped I felt much more satisfied for we're all on the same job so we might as well eat together."

Occasionally, but only occasionally, parcels and their contents were badly beaten up. Stuart Laing reported from a convalescent hospital in England on October 9, 1945 that his last parcel had chased him to Belgium and Holland before it found him. "The cookies were more or less jigsaw puzzle but the taste that a guy dreams about was still there."

The 35 parcels packed on October 26 for Christmas 1943 were representative of everything sent by the Comfort Club. The numbers had steadily increased through 1942 and '43 and would peak at 39 in January of 1945. The experienced packers of the Purchasing and Packing Committee boxed up Klik canned meat, chocolate bars, gum, razor blades, soap and toothpaste. Then came a precious homemade Christmas cake and several dozen cookies, plus a pair of hand-knitted woollen socks and a Christmas card. Wrapped in holiday paper and then in protective wrapping, each box was securely sewn into an old flour sack and the odd Armed Forces address was carefully written on two sides. For $23.28 in postage, the parcels travelled by Canadian Pacific Railway to Regina and east to a ship that would brave the U-boats in the North Atlantic.

What a touch of home those boxes must have carried that winter of 1943, especially in Italy where nine Dilke men were serving at that moment with Canada's Central Mediterranean Forces, seven in fighting units and two with the Royal Canadian Army Medical Corps, patching them up. No parcels reached the battlefront by Christmas, but that didn't matter when the mail call eventually came. The careful packing paid off. "It was in the very best of condition and was enjoyed by myself and the boys," Steve Eberts wrote the day after his box arrived on January 27, 1944.

Lloyd Carr, dug in with the 2nd Armoured Regiment (Lord Strathcona's Horse (Royal Canadians)) outside the medieval town of Ortona on the Adriatic coast, got his parcel February 17. It was enjoyed in a "quite cosy" 10-foot-square slit trench several feet deep with a straw-covered floor and canvas top that housed three men and had some of the comforts of home: "We have a trouble lamp as a light run from our tank and have earphones connected to radio by long wires so can listen in on BBC news etc.," Carr wrote back to Dilke that very day. "We could be worse off, I know, but with mud just outside the door which goes up to your knees pretty well and with Jerry dropping shells all around you, you can pretty well appreciate our comfort."

Whitney Barry and Ted Schultz (Royal Canadian Dragoons of the 1st Armoured Car Regiment and 14th Field Company, Royal Canadian Engineers, respectively) were particularly happy to find woollen socks in their parcels, and Barry asked secretary Mortin to pass on the word that his "fit to a T." "I am sure going to look for a woman who can knit socks like those when I return from overseas," he added. Schultz knew his socks came from Aggie Anfinson, famed throughout the Dilke district for her knitting, and he was especially grateful, he said, because his socks always "grow" holes.

In England, 26 Dilke men received parcels that Christmas. Eight were in the Royal Canadian Air Force, some attached to the Royal Air Force, and the rest in various branches of the army. Gus Koch's box travelled to North Africa before finding him in England just days before Christmas. With RCAF 420 Squadron he had joyfully returned in November from a six-month stint in the desert, his parcel in hot pursuit. Fred Blancheon of the South Saskatchewan Regiment was reminded by his parcel that "[t]hree years ago tonight [December 24, 1940] we docked in a Scottish port fresh as a daisy from Canada, raring to go. But we are still here, but not for long I hope." Butch Side shared his sweets and cakes with English children he had met, and Leo Selinger of the Queen's Own Cameron Highlanders reported that he had been treated to a nice turkey dinner at Christmas "and all the beer I could drink."

Sadly, the committee had struck five names from the list of parcels for Britain. By October 1943, five Dilke volunteers had been killed with the RCAF. Nineteen-year-old Francis Tait, a pilot with 214 Federated Malay States Squadron, was lost during night bombing operations on January 28, 1942, the first of the town's war dead. He was flying as a gunner at the time. Flight Sergeant Observer Francis Dunajski, 23, and the rest of his Halifax crew failed to return from an operation over Kiel, Germany on October 13, 1942. Gunner John Reid, 25, was killed in a training exercise over the North Sea on April 18, 1943. (His army brother Charles says John Reid expected to die in the war. He told people when he left Dilke "that he wasn't going to come back.") Oliver Hills, 22, who was attached to the RAF, was killed on June 23, 1943 in action over Belgium. Gunner Mayson Church, 24, was killed in his Lancaster over Germany on July 30, 1943. Before the war ended, another Dilke son — 22-year-old pilot Allan Silverthorn — would die with the Air Force, on a mission over Siam on June 19, 1945. All these air force dead are remembered on a plaque in Dilke Memorial Hall.

Frank Fuchs was killed in France, fighting with the Regina Rifles shortly after D-Day, and is buried there. For some reason — perhaps because his parents had moved to Regina before the war after years on a farm north of Dilke — his name is not on the memorial plaque, but for the purposes of this book, he, too, is a lost son of Dilke.

*    *    *

One of many such organizations formed during the war, the Dilke Active Service Comfort Club was established to "from time to time send treats to the boys on Active Service from the people of Dilke and District," say the minutes of the founding meeting on October 26, 1940. "From time to time" expanded until, in 1943, "something was sent to each boy every month," the Purchasing and Packing Committee reported. It spent $252.20 for parcel contents that year, 80 percent of it at the three stores in the village: food such as tomato juice and canned meats, other essentials like razor blades and writing paper. Nearly $200 went for cigarettes, chocolates and gum.

It is unfortunately not clear from the minutes how the Comfort Club defined the boys from Dilke and district. Many parcel recipients were young men who went directly into the services from homes in the area. Others had moved away seeking work during the Depression, like the two brothers who had gone from Dilke to Toronto and enlisted there. Their parents continued to live in the village, and perhaps it was that ongoing tie that kept them on the lists for parcels and other treats. In another case, one of two brothers whose family had moved elsewhere in Saskatchewan was considered a "Dilke boy"and was on the list but the other wasn't. This book counts as Dilke people all those to whom the Comfort Club sent parcels, cigarettes, etc., plus others who were raised in the area and had ongoing connections there, for a total of 61 men and one woman who served overseas.

The Comfort Club was registered under the War Charities Act, a battered copy of which survives with three thin exercise books of minutes kept by the three secretaries: popular teacher Ed Schwandt from Strasbourg, who joined the Army and was killed crossing the Seine in 1944; Gwen Bathgate, whose father, hotelier George Daintree, was the first chairman; and Helen Mortin, the author's mother. At the back of each exercise book are long and much-amended lists of service addresses, showing how the Dilke men moved around during their time overseas, sometimes to different regiments or theatres of war. Black boxes are drawn around the final addresses of the dead. Many bills for parcel ingredients purchased from the village's three general stores survive, i.e. $15.71 for 19 packages of cheese at 23 cents, 36 bars at 6 cents, 37 soap at 6 cents and 19 shaving cream at 35 cents each, bought from Side's General Store on March 6, 1944.

Even those prices challenged a club that began life with $14.25 in post-Depression, wartime Saskatchewan. The initial plan to send parcels to all who enlisted from Dilke soon had to be adjusted, and they went only to those serving overseas. But there was great support for the organization. The Ways and Means Committee, charged with raising the money that would pay for everything that was sent, sold nearly 200 25-cent tickets to a community dance on November 22, 1940; that represented one-third of the district's entire population. Admission — a ticket plus 10 cents — included lunch and a chance at three door prizes: 50 pounds of flour, 10 pounds of sugar and a pail of syrup. After the orchestra ($14.00), the hall ($5.00) and other expenses were paid, the dance netted $38.16.

However, costs for the parcels sent overseas for that Christmas totalled $22.01, and more men were shipping out constantly. The Club held more dances but donations, mostly in the $1.00-$2.00 range but some just 25 cents, became its financial lifeline. In March of 1943, when more than 45 Dilke people were in the services, in Canada or overseas, the entire district was canvassed. The money came from individuals — farmer William McLeod is listed on March 2 as making seven $5.00 donations — and from local organizations. A play put on in nearby Findlater raised $20.00. On May 29, 1943, student Millicent Tate (whose father, brother and two sisters were in the forces) handed the Comfort Club $15.00 on behalf of Dilke High School.

Donations made up almost 80 percent of the Club's $658.96 income for the year February 1943 to February 1944, as against expenses of $599.66. The next year, almost $1,000 was raised and $887.45 was spent. Six times that year parcels were packed and cigarettes sent.

"Homemade cookies were included in every parcel," the Purchasing and Packing Committee reported, "and they were excellent cookies, and added to the appreciation the boys felt, as can be seen by the great pile of letters received." Twenty-one families contributed cookies for the 39 parcels sent on January 12, 1945: Anderson, Bathgate, Church, Chypiska, Darby, Gwilym, Hepburn, Holland, Josvanger, Laing, Lipp, MacKay, Metz, Mortin, Nugent, Schmiedge, Selinger, Steif, Tate, Wilton, Zeigler.

Sometimes parcels can be savoured through the letters that came back. On July 28, 1945, Dave Barss, an RCAF gunner who reached England too late to fire a shot, described the receipt of his parcel: "I guess you already know that when one of us gets a parcel over here, there are a half a dozen or more to help open it. It is the same all around so I guess we end up about even." With the most recent Comfort Club offering, "the candy and nuts were attacked first. Later on came the cookies and believe me, they were good. We borrowed some bread and butter from the mess hall last night and had a little snack of cheese and Klik before going to bed. Two of us downed the tomato juice when the rest weren't looking so I guess I got my share if not a little more. The soap and shaving cream I keep for myself which suits me fine because I can always use it." Lloyd Carr's words of nearly two years earlier were still true in 1945: Such sharing "gives each one of us a small touch of our homeland and our dear true friends at home."

Bob Naldrett had been in England nearly three years and would soon be in France with the 14th Canadian Hussars (8th Recce Regiment) when he wrote on April 1, 1944 to thank the Club for chocolates, 300 cigarettes and a parcel: "Surely swell of you people back there to keep on sending these parcels after three or four years. It is so easy to forget, but Dilke don't appear to be the forgetting kind. So many of the chaps over here do seem to have been forgotten that it makes me feel quite proud."

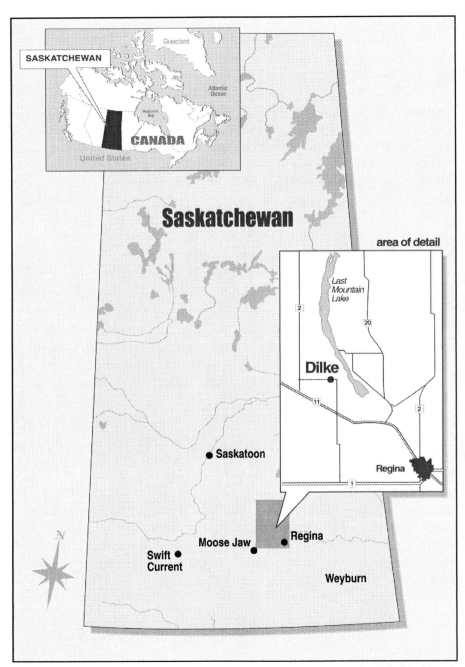

# II.

# They Went from Dilke

Tiny Dilke was a splendid hometown in the 1930s and '40s. It was small, so everyone knew and helped each other in the traditional rural way. Most joined in or at least attended the many activities: sports — baseball and hockey primarily, but tennis lovers had courts to play on right beside the main street — and musical and dramatic presentations. Its school was well-attended, as were its churches, and Saturday night was a big occasion every week. The many children were known and watched out for by everyone in the community as they grew into adulthood. Nostalgia for the village seeps through the lines of many of the letters written by those one-time children back to the Comfort Club throughout the war. "Hoping that before another year is out we shall all have the privilege of attending a dance in the I.O.O.F. hall once again," Art Boehme wrote optimistically from RCAF 419 Squadron on December 18, 1943. "I would not mind pulling into Dilke for one of those good old Saturday nights we used to have," Fred Blancheon said six weeks before he landed in Normandy in 1944 with the South Saskatchewan Regiment. With the end of the war in Europe in sight, Walter Tate was in Holland, a driver-batman with RCAF 666 Air Observation Post squadron and eager for home, even though he expected to find it much changed: "Still, I can hardly wait to see everyone again."

During arguments and chatter with his workmates at RCAF 431 heavy bomber squadron in Yorkshire, Leading Aircraftman Reece

Jones was ribbed about coming from "a little one-horse town among the sand hills and gophers," he wrote on March 7, 1945. "But I always answer back by saying that the people that live there are thoughtful enough to send me parcels, that's more than the folks in their big cities will do." Bert Tait, who had turned 21 as he sailed for England, thought his hometown also did more than neighbouring communities of similar size. Eight men from four nearby villages were serving with him and three other Dilke men in 8th Recce Regiment, he wrote on July 21, 1943: "We get together and discuss the news and parcels that we get and I believe Dilke does more for us than the other towns do for their hometown boys."

Fighter pilot Tom Koch was still happy in England after 2½ years, he wrote on February 22, 1944, "but there are times when I would like to get back to see all the folks around Dilke and its neighbouring districts. The changes since I left have been many, and sometimes I think I don't want to go back because it isn't the same place that I left, the place that I have dreamed of away from home, but then I think of the people. They are still there, or most of them at least — the young have grown old, and the old people are older. New families have sprung up, and the children that I knew are young men and women now. Maybe the changes aren't so great and it is only time that has marched on, but before I get back, I hope that time has brought the peace we are fighting for."

Though his family lived in Dilke only from 1927 to 1946, "that's home, still," Sam Side said during an interview 54 years later. Prominent in his home office in Dawson Creek, British Columbia is a photo of a handful of young Dilke boys celebrating a birthday party, Sam Side and younger brother Butch in their midst. "Dilke was very much a great place to grow up, and they all turned out well and successful."

*    *    *

The first settlers arrived about 1881 in the prairie region that would become Dilke and district, in the Last Mountain Valley in south-central Saskatchewan. The village perched above a wide, deep ravine that meandered east about five miles to Last Mountain Lake, which cuts its way north-south on the great plains like a long east-facing apostrophe. The 1941 census counted 575 people in Dilke and the farming areas it served. Three general stores, three churches, one school, a hotel and beer parlour, a livery barn and a garage pretty well made up the business district. Most of the buildings spread along Main Street parallel to the Canadian Pacific Railway and the four adjacent grain elevators. Highway 11 passed by just to the south, but has since moved.

Ninety-two men and nine women from Dilke and district joined Canada's services during the Second World War. About 12 percent of those were living and working elsewhere when they enlisted, including two who were teaching school. Many of those who went directly from Dilke were farming with their families, or just out of school. Nine months after Canada declared war on September 10, 1939, Edward MacKay, Ivan McEwen and Alan Wilton had enlisted in the army, according to the Dilke column in the *Craik Weekly News* of May 2, 1940. MacKay later switched to the RCAF and became a pilot, but while he was in the army he met King George and Queen Elizabeth when they reviewed Canadian troops in England. There's a touch of envy in Fred Blancheon's reference to this meeting in his third letter to the Comfort Club, written in July 1941 and carried in its entirety in the weekly paper. "I hear Ted MacKay had the pleasure of talking to the King and Queen for a few minutes. They spoke briefly to a few of our boys" — he was in the South Saskatchewan Regiment — "but this is a pretty big outfit to inspect. I guess we have about as many officers and sergeant-majors as there are men in Ted's outfit." MacKay and Wilton were serving in the 2nd Canadian Anti-Tank Regiment. "I wish I had joined in with Ted and Al," Blancheon added sadly. "All of the Dilke boys should have been together."

At least 25 Dilke men were in uniform by the end of 1940, most of them still in Canada. Four were in England, and the Comfort Club formed in late October of that year mailed sizable Christmas boxes to each of them. In February it was gearing up to send seven parcels as more and more Canadians crossed the ocean to Britain.

Like young men across Canada, the "boys from Dilke" enlisted out of duty and patriotism, longing for adventure and/or hope for gainful employment after the lack of opportunities in the Depression, sometimes just for the promise of a new and different life. In the summer of 1941, 18-year-old Butch Side was sent by his father to farm six sections of land between Dilke and a nearby village for $20 a month. He wasn't exactly enthusiastic about his dawn-to-dark labours, he recalled 58 years later. "Come fall after the crop is complete and everything is all done and I was paid all my money, I went to Regina. I drove Dad's truck to pick up a load of stuff [to take] out to the store (his parents ran a general store in Dilke) and would you believe I joined the services. I took my truck all loaded with food and everything else and put it into one of the places Dad went to, and I just said, 'I joined the services,' and Dad had to go pick it up ... He was madder than hell."

More than anything, Side said, he joined the Army on September 24, 1941 to escape farming and working in the store. "It was better than what I was doing, and it wasn't that bad. I enjoyed it." The son of immigrants from what is now Lebanon, he was eager to fight for Canada, but the army trained him as a clerk-stenographer at the Saskatoon Technical High School. "They felt I was young enough and probably smart enough and they wanted me to become one and I says 'Okay'." He remembers that he wasn't allowed to go overseas until he was 20; he sailed in mid-October 1943 with the Canadian Armoured Corps Reinforcement Unit. Plans for him to go to the Italian campaign were defeated by his flat feet, and he was stationed in southern England throughout the war. Eventually, promoted to sergeant, he helped organize troops' return to Canada.

Joe Ell was teaching during the 1941-42 school year, but after Pearl Harbor, he remembers, "I thought, boy, it's time, I got to get into this because sooner or later I'm going to get a call and I should be there anyway." He resigned at the end of June and joined the RCAF in Regina, getting his wings in Portage la Prairie, Manitoba as a bomb aimer and photographer.

Gus Koch remembers being influenced to enlist in the RCAF by "the horrible stories we heard that were going on in Europe ... and there was help needed. Canada was a dominion of the empire and I would say there was quite a calling to respond." But he also remembers that "when you were brought up during the Depo years and the hardships, you always looked around for something you enjoyed doing and could do. And I was very, very interested in mechanics. I had been taking a correspondence course in diesel mechanics with National Schools of Los Angeles when I joined up so that sort of set the stage for what I was going to be involved with." He did try for air crew when he enlisted, however. "The thing is, when they read what I had been doing, they said, No, you'd make a good aero-engine mechanic. Chap behind me came from Rouleau, his parents had a pharmacy, he wanted to be a pharmacist. No, he'd be a good mechanic. Guy from Winnipeg, his parents had a store, he wanted to be in stores, no, he'd make a real good mechanic. There was real need for mechanics because at that time they were forming 6 Bomber Group in England, with multi-engine aircraft, and they needed many, many mechanics." He was allotted to 420 (Snowy Owl) Squadron, which would take him to North Africa.

The RCAF was the first choice of Charles Reid, Lloyd Carr and Steve Eberts, too, but all three ended up in the army. RCAF recruiters said Reid, who farmed with his father, would not be able to get time off for harvest; the army was more understanding. He chose tanks and served in the 9th Armoured Regiment, the British Columbia Dragoons, in Italy and Europe. Carr and Eberts didn't meet the air force's earliest recruiting requirements and opted for the army; the former ended up in tanks, the latter a gunner. Looking back, Carr says his enlistment in September 1940 was both his duty and "something I wanted to do .... Of course I was an adventurous type of person to start with." More than a year in Italy would wipe out some of that love of adventure. Eberts was farming with his parents and looking for change, and he, too, found that change on the Mediterranean front.

Albert Horne's farm family was "basically kind of against the war," he recalls, his father inclined to pacifism. He was 20 when his stepmother said one day, "I guess it looks like nobody from our family is going to go." He's not sure that influenced him to volunteer for the RCAF in 1941, "but I expect it did." Thwarted by his eyesight from his first choice, air gunnery, he opted to become an aero-engine mechanic. After a pre-enlistment course in Regina, he trained in Brandon, Manitoba and St. Thomas, Ontario and was posted to 434 Squadron (heavy bombers) based at Tholthorpe and then at Croft, England.

Nobody joined for the money, but after the Depression a sure $1 a day was not a bad rate of pay. No one could draw the entire pay cheque, Gus Koch remembers, for some of it went to the families at home. Single men had to allot a certain percentage of the pay to their parents. The families of married men got most of their pay. "You got spending money and that's really about all you needed. Everything else was found. Your health, your clothes, your lodging, everything was found." Butch Side remembers that after he was promoted to sergeant, he had to send $20 a month home to his mother in Dilke.

Of the 101 Dilke men and women who joined Canada's wartime forces, just four served in the Navy, surprising in light of the prairies' reputation for producing sailors. Thirty-nine joined the RCAF, 32 men as air or ground crew and seven in the Women's Division. Two women served with the Canadian Women's Army Corps, and two First World War veterans joined the Veterans Guard. Three men served in the Army Medical Corps and one in the U.S. army. The list of Canadian Army postings is led in numbers by 8th Reconnaissance and the South Saskatchewan Regiments. Dilke men were in tanks, in the engineers and the artillery, in armoured cars and in the infantry. They were sappers, gunners, dragoons, riflemen, clerks; two played in Army orchestras in Britain. One ended up as a commando attached to the British Army.

Beginning in 1940 and stretching well into 1946, 62 Dilke people served overseas, representing their little village in North Africa and the Mediterranean theatres, in Europe, in the North Atlantic and in the skies over Asia. Thirty-five were in various branches of the army, four in the navy and 20 in the air force, including, in its Women's Division, Regina Eberts, the only woman from Dilke who went overseas; she was posted to London for nearly two years. Two Dilke men were medics and one was in the Veterans Guard in London until late in 1943. Several were in the Canadian Army Occupation Force, and a handful were prepared to carry on to the war with Japan, though it ended before they could leave Canada for the second time.

Enlisting seemed to be a family thing. All four children of Harry and Margaret Wilton served, James in the 1st Survey Regiment, Alan in an anti-tank regiment, Lenore in RCAF Women's Division and Walter, the youngest, in the navy. Four sons of Joseph and Sarah Tait joined the air force; Francis, 19, who planned to become a doctor, was killed during night bombing operations in January 1942, the first and youngest of Dilke's war dead. Three sons of Peter and Theresa Fuchs spread themselves among the three services; Frank, 21, was killed shortly after D-Day. (Another Fuchs son, the youngest, had been called to go when the war ended.) Jack Tate, who emigrated from England in 1914 and returned almost at once with the Canadian Infantry Brigade to fight in the First World War, went back again in 1940 with the Veterans Guard and was stationed in London. His son Walter joined the artillery at the same time, and daughters Dorothy and Joan spent two years in the RCAF Women's Division. Two sons and a daughter of Alex and Latifa Side enlisted, in the RCAF, the army and the Canadian Women's Army Corps. The families of James and Nancy Barry, Joe and Margareta Koch and John and Johanna Dunajski each contributed three sons to the army and the air force. Teacher Francis Dunajski, who left the classroom for the air force on March 31, 1941, was reported missing in air operations over Germany in October 1942, less than five months after he went overseas; he was 23.

Seven men from Dilke were killed: Mayson Church, Francis Dunajski, Oliver Hills, John Reid, Allan Silverthorn and Francis Tait with the air force, and Frank Fuchs with the army. The RCAF dead represent almost half of those who flew as aircrew. Four were killed on bombing missions over Europe, one in action over Siam, one in a training accident over the North Sea. Church is buried in Germany and Hills in Belgium; Dunajski, Reid and Tait have no known graves and their names are engraved on the Runnymede War Memorial at Surrey in England. Silverthorn's name is inscribed on the Singapore War Memorial in Malaya. Fuchs was killed in France three days after he landed on D-Day with the Regina Rifles, and he is buried near Courseules-sur-Mer. Eleven men were wounded serving with the army, so the casualties represent half of those who were in combat. One soldier lost an eye and a hand in a workshop accident while training in England, and another was discharged while still in Canada after a knee injury received during training that affected his walk for the rest of his life. One RCAF recruit received a medical discharge while still in Canada. In total, fatal and non-fatal casualties represent 21 percent of the Dilke men and women who enlisted, and exactly one-third of those who served overseas.

The long address lists in the rear of the Comfort Club minute books show that three Dilke soldiers earned commissions as lieutenants: Ernest Barry in the Cape Breton Highlanders, before he shifted to the commandos; Harold Buck in No. 2 Canadian Base Reinforcement Group and Jim Wilton in the Canadian Army Reinforcement Unit. Lloyd Carr in the Lord Strathcona's Horse, Butch Side in the Canadian Armoured Corps Reinforcement Unit, Alan Wilton, 2nd Anti-Tank Regiment, and Pete Thauberger, 3rd Canadian Field Survey Company, became sergeants. Walter Tate was a lance-sergeant in the artillery in 1943 but was demoted to gunner late in the year "for staying out at night like a bad boy," he wrote home. "The 'Old Man' took a dim view of it." Ed Brandon rose to corporal in France with the Royal Winnipeg Rifles. In the air force, fighter pilot Tom Koch was commissioned as a flight lieutenant, Joe Ell as a flying officer and Alexander Fuchs and Allan Silverthorn as pilot officers. Sam Side, John Reid, Mayson Church, Oliver Hills, Francis Dunajski and Francis Tait were all flight sergeants. Among ground crew, George Tait rose to sergeant and Reece Jones to corporal.

Two RCAF airmen received medals, Joe Ell the Distinguished Flying Cross and Alexander Fuchs the Czech Medal for Valour. Art Boehme and Gus Koch, in ground crew, earned mention in despatches.

During their years and years of preparation and work in Britain, 10 Dilke men found wives. Fred Blancheon remained in Derby, England with his wife after the war, but Dave Barss, Gus Koch, Reece Jones, Jack Naldrett, Lawrence Smith, Pete Thauberger and Alan Wilton brought their English and Scottish wives — sometimes with children — back to Canada and some of them settled in the Dilke district. Ernest "Happy" Burns and his wife came to Canada and then returned to England. In 1947, Kitty Forsyth of Glasgow, Scotland came to Saskatchewan to marry Clarence Wray, and they farmed near Findlater, not far from Dilke, until his death in 1950.

Most of the men and women from Dilke who went overseas during the Second World War are dead now, but they live on in the freshness of their youth and unique experiences through their letters to the Comfort Club. In the memories of those who survive, the Club signifies the enduring love of the little prairie town they still call home.

# III.

# DILKE IN ENGLAND — THE ARMY

A S FAST as they could be packed into the ships, men from every part of Canada poured into Britain. "Everywhere you go you see Canadians," Fred Blancheon wrote to the Comfort Club in late 1941, and more were arriving constantly. Among them was a steady stream from Dilke. "I've seen so many boys I know that England is beginning to look like home," Ted Schultz of engineers' 4 Field Company wrote that October.

For most of these men, the road to war was so long and slow that there was plenty of time to meet friends from home, explore England and Scotland and learn the local ways. After the rough edges had been rubbed off in Canada, most Dilke soldiers endured up to three years of training in Britain, interspersed with garrison duty and/or coastal defence. They were eager to get at the job they had left home to do, but most would have no opportunity until D-Day or soon after. But for a small group, war became reality much sooner. On August 19, 1942, three Dilke men — Fred Blancheon and Ed Brandon of the South Saskatchewan Regiment and Leo Selinger of the Queen's Own Cameron Highlanders of Canada — were among the Canadians who tested the German defences in the Dieppe Raid. They had been in England for a year and more. Others met the reality of war in Sicily and/or Italy in 1943. Clarence Wray had been preparing for three years, Ted Schultz for two and a half, when they headed for the Mediterranean arena, but Steve Eberts, Lloyd Carr, Charles Reid, Whitney Barry and Dean Amberson shipped south after only months in Britain, barely time to get used to the accent. We shall follow them in Chapter VI.

For most of those from Dilke, this was their first experience away from home and they dug right in. Bob Naldrett of 8th Recce Regiment had acquired "quite the English accent and mannerisms of speech" after a year and a half, he wrote on March 22, 1943. "You will hardly be able to understand us when we return, and some of the expressions we use will probably shock you too, though uttered quite unwittingly by us. We had many a laugh from their expressions, but are acclimatized now." Fred Blancheon was an English immigrant who had been working as a hired man on a farm near Dilke before enlisting in the SSR. He reported on March 18, 1941 that the Canadians were settling down to English ways. "I found it hard to get on to their ways and I was born here," he added. He intended to spend his second leave seeing old school chums. Four months later, while thanking the Comfort Club for the cigarettes he had recently received, he added, "Now if you can only move a big restaurant and hot dog stand over here, that would really fix us all right. About all we can get in a café is beans on toast and of course we have fish and chips shops all over the country, but it takes a big supply to feed us." It's likely he never did warm to beans on toast, for two years later he wrote that the Comfort Club could never imagine how its parcels were appreciated. "We get tired of beans on toast at our canteen, but they do change it once in a while to toast on beans."

It was the potatoes that got Reece Jones down. "They feed us potatoes three times a day," he wrote from the Yorkshire base of 431 Squadron in April 1943. "After this war none of us will be able to look a potato square in the face. We grumble and grouch but things could be far worse and likely will be before the trouble is cleared."

After the waiting and the eternal preparation for action that never came, food and cigarettes were the biggest complaints about life in Britain, and the Comfort Club was often a lifesaver. His latest parcel had arrived very opportunely, Bob Naldrett wrote in March 1943. His section of 8th Recce Regiment was just off on a two-week training scheme "so the honey and cheese came in very handy for a quick lunch. After a strenuous day's drive, the raisins nearly saved my driver and I from starvation one night. We had breakfast about 6 a.m. and just before dinner got orders to move and were driving off and on until 10 p.m. without a stop being made for food. We were nearly starved but about 7 p.m. I happened to think of the bag of raisins I had saved from your parcel. We enjoyed everything that was in that parcel, but nothing compared with the satisfaction we got out of that bag of raisins. We offered up a prayer of thanks to you ladies with every raisin."

He had a swell time on that scheme, Naldrett went on, with sunshine every day and lots of action and excitement to make things interesting. "Lots of farmers haven't as many chickens and eggs as they had previous to the scheme," he admitted, "but the Army must be fed and the Canadian Army are quite adept at taking care of themselves. Interesting incidents arose that we still get a laugh out of. For instance, one of my chums was transferred to a tank regiment for duration of the scheme. One day they were driving down the road and the driver failed to make a turn ... and went slam bang into a brick house, practically demolishing it. An elderly couple lived in the house and came out quite shaken but unhurt, the old lady, however, wringing her hands and wailing, 'My poor Budgy. Someone save my Budgy.' The chaps in the tank immediately jumped to the conclusion there was someone trapped in the house, possibly a boy or girl, and started to dig frantically in the debris. They had just about moved every brick and timber when a neighbour of the old couple came along and explained 'Budgy' was a bird. They discovered 'Budgy' sitting on a shelf quite unconcerned. They retrieved him to the old lady, who was overjoyed, quite unconcerned about her home being smashed up so long as 'Budgy' was safe."

Schemes weren't always interesting or amusing. Two SSR sergeants and a private were killed by a grenade on a training scheme in early May of 1943, Fred Blancheon reported. Another man was shot and given only a 50-50 chance of living. "There'll be a big funeral tomorrow, some of the boys are coming in off the scheme to attend it."

Charles Ell remembers the men from Dilke as naive country boys who were often taken advantage of. "We believed everything we heard. For instance, when we first joined up, they'd say, 'Anybody that can drive a truck, fall out over here.' Of course, most of the boys would prefer driving truck in those days to anything else so there'd be half-a-dozen boys fall out, presumably to be truck drivers. And the corporal would say, 'Okay, you and you follow me' and you would peel potatoes for the rest of the day ... That was one example of how naive we were, we'd believe anything because at home we'd been taught to respect people."

They shifted here and there around Britain. Gunner Clarence Wray counted up 16 moves in a letter in February 1941, commenting, "The time seems to pass much faster when we see new surroundings." Fred Blancheon and the SSR moved three times in just under a year. "The best place we were in was on the south coast. We had a wonderful six weeks there and hated to leave but we may go back again soon so we are hoping for the best." This was no beach holiday. Canadian regiments were sent to guard the English coast against possible invasion. "England sure has a wonderful fortress to protect her. Some of the guns here would blow Dilke off the map. We can see them in the cliffs." The regiment built a lot of roads there, he wrote on June 11, 1942.

Gunner Alan Wilton's 2nd Anti-Tank Regiment was the first to be assigned to coastal duty, he wrote in a letter published in *The Craik Weekly News* on August 18, 1941: "I have been swimming in the sea quite a bit lately. We are right in a city and is it ever swell here and the people are so awfully good to us. They bring us tea about a dozen times a day. I have been here for two weeks. We are the first Canadians to be here and I was in the advance party so got well established before the rest of the gang got here. I don't know how long we will be here but hope it is quite a while. It is just heaven compared to Aldershot." Alas, his time in paradise was short. In September he wrote that the five weeks on coastal guard — "but it was more like a leave" — were up and they were back at Aldershot, "and even to the same billets."

Aldershot, home of the British Army for nearly a century, became the main Canadian Army base after British troops departed for the Continent in 1939. Charles Ell remembers it as a holding unit for overseas troops. In an interview that took place exactly 50 years after he sailed with the Ordnance Corps from Halifax aboard the *Capetown Castle*, he recalled that all Canadian units went to Aldershot before being distributed to the regions of Britain. He arrived there the day of the Dieppe Raid. "We travelled by rail to Aldershot where most of the veterans, the soldiers that had been to Dieppe, had left from the day before. The next morning, the people that were left of that raid came back — a few of them — and we assumed we were next."

Among those few who came back from Dieppe were Dilke's Fred Blancheon and Ed Brandon (South Saskatchewan Regiment) and Leo Selinger (Queen's Own Cameron Highlanders of Canada). Blancheon wrote regularly to the Comfort Club throughout his five years with the army, 32 letters in all. He was silent only from June 11, 1942, two months before Dieppe, to March 8, 1943. Selinger wrote no letters before December 1943. Brandon's few letters don't even hint at Dieppe.

Four simultaneous attacks along roughly 12 miles of coast near Dieppe were planned for August 19, 1942, according to a history written by Cecil Law (an acting lance-sergeant in the Highland Sea-forths of Canada in 1942) and posted on the website cap.estevan.sk.ca, which devotes much attention to the raid. (Nearby Weyburn was the home of the South Saskatchewan Regiment). Law says the Canadians were chosen for this adventure "because they were as yet un-blooded, were becoming restless, and had a reputation from the First World War for bold and dashing action in the attack." As well as the SSR and the Camerons, the Royal Regiment of Canada, the Royal Hamilton Light Infantry, the Essex Scottish, the 14th Canadian Army Tank Regiment (the Calgary Tanks) and No. 4 and No. 3 (British) Commando took part. The immediate reserve force was Les Fusiliers Mont-Royal and the Royal Marines "A" Commando.

The town of Pourville, two miles west of Dieppe, was the attack point for the regiments with Dilke men, the SSR and the Camerons. The South Saskatchewan was to land on Green Beach opposite Pourville and secure it with minimum delay to enable the Camerons, landing 30 minutes later, to pass through without opposition. The Camerons were then to push beyond the town and join the Calgary Tanks and the Royal Hamilton Light Infantry to attack the airfield at Arques-la-Bataille and then the German Divisional Headquarters farther inland. "These tasks would have been impossible for any troop in the Second World War," says the Veterans Affairs Canada website on Dieppe. The SSR was to clear the town, especially a farmhouse on the high ground, the Farm of the Four Winds. That was the plan; the reality, as we know, was much different.

Most of the SSR was mistakenly landed on the west side of the Scie River which flowed through the centre of Green Beach, and so had much farther to go to begin their task. Luckily, they landed without opposition at about 4.50 a.m., but that was the last of their luck. Resistance stiffened as they crossed the Scie and pushed toward Dieppe, and they were soon under constant heavy fire. They were stopped well short of the town, but the Camerons pushed on more than a mile toward their airfield target before they too were halted. Returning to the beaches and the ships waiting there took another large toll. In all, 907 Canadians lost their lives in six hours on the beaches and fields around Dieppe, including 84 from the SSR and 76 Camerons. The Germans took 1,946 prisoners. Less than half of the 4,963 who had embarked that morning returned to England, and many of those were wounded. Among the wounded was Fred Blancheon of Dilke. SSR commander Lieutenant-Colonel C.C.I. Merritt won the Victoria Cross for his courage in leading his men across the bridge over the Scie under heavy fire and for other heroic acts, the first Canadian VC of the Second World War.

Blancheon, who had married just 11 days before he went to France, took a while to recover from the events of August 19. "I have not been the best since the raid," he wrote on May 18, 1943, "but have got myself an easy job in the stores." He never quite lost his enthusiasm. On July 15, when the Allies were fighting in Sicily and the South Saskatchewan Regiment was trooping the colours in London, he wrote, "The Canadians are really doing good in Sicily, wait till our bunch go to Berlin, it will be about the size of Dilke when we get through with it."

Almost two months later, he was not feeling so good about serving with the SSR. "I am trying to get out of the Regiment," he wrote on September 12. "In a way I hate to leave it as I have seen action with it, but us old boys seem to get the rough end of the deal now. To tell you the truth, we are strangers in the Regiment we formed up in Weyburn. It is kind of moral[e] breaking to us, but what can we do, all we hope for is action, it will kind of straighten things out." The following July, he and the South Saskatchewan Regiment returned to France.

*    *    *

The joy with which Dilke men received a box of 300 Sweet Caporal cigarettes from home seems almost shocking now, with all we know about the perils of smoking, "They are a very valued gift," Bob Naldrett wrote in November 1941, when cigarettes were hard to come by. "Even the canteens cannot supply the demand. In our own particular canteen we were allowed to buy five cigarettes at one time for several weeks. Lately though, they have increased that ration to 10. Even then, they are all English brands and contain far more 'filler' than tobacco." Fred Blancheon wrote that he was paying about 40 cents an ounce for tobacco "and as we draw half pay now it sure makes a hole in the pay. I guess we'll have to quit smoking."

Obviously no one took that idea seriously. Four years later, Gunnar Gustafson wrote from No. 1 Canadian Signals Reinforcement Unit, "You would have enjoyed yourselves had you been able to be present and heard all the boys saying 'Well, we smoke again' as I walked the length of our hut with my prize package under my arm. I believe this is the first bunch of cigarettes any of our bunch have received ... I can assure you that a good Canadian cigarette was very welcome." The feeling was widespread. "A Sweet Caporal cigarette is most desirable after landing," fighter pilot Tom Koch explained, "especially if the trip has been exciting and full of nervous tension. Also, while waiting long hours at dispersal for takeoff, a great number of cigarettes are smoked to help occupy the mind and fingers, so the constant supply of cigarettes is highly appreciated." And if like Lloyd Smith you happened not to smoke, cigarettes could be traded for whisky.

Inconceivable as it seems today, even the Red Cross supplied cigarettes. In November 1944, Leo Selinger wrote from 24 Canadian General Hospital that he had received the Comfort Club's cigarette contribution the day before. He had been waiting a long time, he said, but the need was not so great "as the Red Cross has been keeping everybody with 50 cigs a week, but you know when a fellow lays around all day with nothing to do he's usually killing time with a cig lit.

I've been fortunate enough to manage to get some from some of the boys around here. As for buying English cigs, well I'll probably have to stop smoking before my pocketbook gets too low."

They turned to local cigarettes only in desperation. "A fellow doesn't realize how much they [the Canadian brand] mean until he has to smoke a few of these English cigarettes which have no comparison at all," Frank Koch of RCAF 415 Squadron wrote in 1944. They had no taste, no bite, but made up for that in price. In April 1943, Jack Tate, based in London with the Veterans Guard, said cigarette tax had been raised and shops now charged 45 cents for 20. In Yorkshire with RCAF 431 Squadron, Reece Jones was paying 56 cents for 20. The Comfort Club paid $1 for a carton of 300 Sweet Caporals sent directly to England from the manufacturer.

Its cigarettes aside, Britain's countryside, the wonders of its cities, the friendliness of its people made the years of waiting bearable and even pleasant for the men from Dilke. They knew they were having the opportunity of their lives. "There's one thing about this war ... we get to see places we would certainly never see otherwise," Charles Reid spoke for them all in September 1943, a few months before embarking for Italy with the British Columbia Dragoons. "I was in Edinburgh for a while and then went down to London for a couple of days."

The travel was the best part of life in Britain, Butch Side remembers. Canadian soldiers were quick to take advantage of their free train travel around a compact island and leaves that could be as short as a day or a weekend or as long as two weeks. In the 13 months from August 1942, Art Boehme visited Scotland, staying at a private home in Edinburgh for almost a week; London for 10 days, taking in the latest shows and a concert at the "wonderful" Royal Albert Hall; Liverpool with a 45-mile weekend cycling trip to North Wales through countryside that was "a mass of flowers, especially buttercups and daisies"; and the south of England by truck, passing through Windsor with its castle, "really a huge place built on a hill."

In March of 1945, Gunnar Gustafson reported on three days in Scotland in which he "saw the famous Clyde and its shipbuilding, went skating and saw a performance of ice dancing which was really very good, went on a factory tour consisting of a factory for boots & shoes, jams & jellies, drugs, paper & printing, all sorts of tins for canned foods etc., and also fabrics." Going on to London, he packed in the Houses of Parliament, Big Ben, Victoria Tower, Westminster Bridge, St. Margaret's Church, Westminster Abbey, Buckingham Palace, Madam Tussaud's, St. James Park, Admiralty Arch, 10 Downing Street, Whitehall, St. Thomas Hospital, Hyde Park, Trafalgar Square and Piccadilly Circus, where, he said, the commandos hung out. In the courts he saw "the judges and lawyers with their curly wigs." He found people were still sleeping in the underground stations.

London was by far the biggest city men from Dilke had ever seen. Joe Ell calls it the highlight of his travels in Britain, and Frank Selinger found it a great learning experience. "The Tower of London interested me most," wrote Selinger, who reached England in 1945 and was soon busy interpreting from German to English. "There lived nearly all the rulers of England. What teachers had been trying to drive into my skull in public school became very realistic that day. It was the best review of British history I've ever had."

But they travelled far beyond London. Jack Klein spent a happy nine-day leave in Leeds. Ted Schultz paid several visits to Stratford-on-Avon, and on his second trip combined a play at the Shakespeare Memorial Theatre with fishing in the Avon. Stuart Laing had two great leaves in Scotland — "what you might call heaven compared to this," he wrote later from the front in Germany — where he was welcomed by relatives on both sides of his family. Clarence Wray stayed in Glasgow with sisters of a friend in Saskatchewan. Butch Side went to Manchester to meet his brother Sam, who was en route home to Canada in February 1945, and they lived it up.

Charles Ell remembers that "every leave we tried to go some place new." He spent two weeks at Balliol College in Oxford. "It was neat because we just sat in with the students and listened to the lectures and we didn't have to write exams, of course. And we ate with the men. I was surprised that every evening when they ate they'd have a tankard of ale, and I thought, Oh, this was great." Each night he put his shoes outside his cubicle and in the morning they were gleaming. That was a unique experience, but he also remembers having a wonderful time with pilot Tom Koch in Aberdeen, Scotland, a white city built on granite.

It was the country beyond the cities that most impressed Frank Selinger. "England's countryside is very beautiful," he wrote in June of 1945. "Many people at home simply admire the few flowers, the odd clump of trees and the hedges here and there. Over here Mother Nature is much different. Every little field, every house, every roadside is surrounded and adorned with various kinds of flowers, trees and shrubs. People don't go car riding even if they do have plenty of petrol. They walk to enjoy the countryside. I've seen nearly all of southern England. It's one mass of beauty."

He would still take Canada, however. "Home is home, be it only a piano-box."

*     *     *

It wasn't a piano but a saxophone and a typewriter that made Charles Ell's stint in the Ordnance Corps the turning point in his life. The typewriter was his workaday instrument for his job at No. 1 Base Ordnance Depot in Borden, Hampshire, where he handled the paperwork that accompanied the materièl that came into the depot and was then requisitioned. "It changed my life," he says now. "It took me away from the farm and I had a chance to learn the type of work that they used in an office." Borden became almost like home, 20 men or so tightly packed into a Nissen hut with a potbellied stove in the middle. They would make a fire at night with coal they had scrounged and toast bread, also scrounged, by sticking the pieces on the stove. "When they fell off, they were done."

Many and many a night Ell missed this midnight snack because of his second job, playing in an army dance band. He had picked up the sax at home, well enough to be recruited for the band, but now he learned to read music. "We played orchestrations which meant you had to learn to play your part, whereas previously we just played maybe the melody and a little bit of harmony. In orchestrations if you didn't play your part, there was a hole in the music and you'd be put out in a hurry." Music was his salvation, he believes, and certainly more fun than his job.

In a band hut out in the trees away from the rest of the camp, they could practise as much as they wanted. Ell learned to play other instruments, including the bass and the trombone. "The instruments were all there, and we had the benefit of good tuition, too." They travelled in a special band truck to engagements in London or a wide area around the city, in big halls or officers' clubs, from 1942 through 1945. At one dance in London, the band couldn't compete with the bombs and the ack-ack; the air raid wardens shut the dance down. It seemed like great fun when they got out on the street, Ell remembers, until he noticed a big hotel burning. Its name, the Regina, brought the war sharply home to a man from Saskatchewan. As a general rule, however, bombing was so common that the musicians paid little attention, except when they made their way through the darkness of the blackout.

Everybody was dancing to the great swing music of the era, Ell remembers. "It was the big escape and it was a morale builder, too. I guess that's why they kept me on, because one of the big things was to keep the troops entertained and to help morale." He realizes now that this was a considerable contribution to the war effort, though that didn't occur to him at the time. "We were doing what we loved and getting paid for it. We got a pound a night, that was five dollars, you know. Soldiers got one dollar a day." After the armistice, the band played "every night because it was just one big jamboree ... everybody wanted to celebrate."

The most frightening thing he experienced was the buzz bombs; before that he had no sense of danger. "They sounded like a motorcycle engine, only there was a trail of fire about 10 feet behind the buzz bomb and as long as it kept going, you knew .... because once the motor cut out, there was a gradual descent. So if it was over top of you and the motor was still going, you were safe. That was a scary weapon. I think people were more afraid of the buzz bombs than anything else." He remembers the V1 rockets — "you would hear the explosion and then you would hear the rocket coming, they travelled at faster than the speed of sound. They were scary. If you heard it, it was too late."

Such danger quickly became the normal accompaniment to life in Britain for the men from Dilke. "We hear the mournful wailings of the sirens pretty nearly every night," Fred Blancheon of the SSR wrote in

May 1941, adding, as only a prairie boy could, "It sounds like a coyote some times." Bombs were falling as he wrote, leading him to comment about "the hell people over here have to go through just because one man wants to own the world. If I get a chance of meeting him (which of course is not likely), I think I would try hard for a bulls eye." On December 24, 1943, he reported that his new English wife found the air raids at the base much worse than she was used to. He had advised her to do what the Canadians do: "Just swear a little and roll over and go to sleep."

In February 1944, Butch Side described for the folks at home just what went on during a raid. "Firstly, as in all raids it's usually pitch black and of course the alert is given by means of the siren wails and [we] can hear the Jerries coming in the distance but [it] sure doesn't take long to come in over the area we're in. The searchlights go on everywhere, then the ack-ack guns start giving the reception and when the shells explode in the sky they give off beautiful light (I presume the Huns don't like it). We have the new rocket guns going and it sends up an explosive which is a sensational and most magnificent sight of all, it leaves a red line all the way up ... and when it explodes it also gives a red glow lighting the area. In the meantime, the Jerries are dropping flares of all colours and description lighting up the entire area (these of course come down in parachutes). They also drop concentrated amounts of this anti-radio location paper, which I'm enclosing, which disturbs radios etc. by absorbing radio frequency alternating currents and changing them." The odd plane comes down and a few bombs "shake the dust off good old mother earth."

Just 18 when he enlisted on September 24, 1941, Side was trained by the Army as a clerk-stenographer and a wireless operator, and sent overseas in October 1943. He sailed on the crowded *Aquitania*, where they slept in layers of four. "Everybody got crabs," he remembers. "It didn't matter whether you knew them or not, they kind of fell on you." He was training to go to Sicily and/or Italy as a wireless operator with the Governor-General's Horse Guards, but heavily-loaded route marches of 20 to 25 miles showed up his flat feet and the regiment left without him. He was assigned to Records in a reinforcement unit, sending casualties home and replacements to the fronts, which became a busy job as the war expanded to Western Europe. He had to keep track of where soldiers were sent, and when, if they had gone missing or were imprisoned. Although based at Aldershot or nearby Woking, he was often on the move. Occasionally he was sent to Canadian headquarters in London, and during one such visit he sheltered with others under a stairway as a buzz bomb exploded a nearby watertank. "We slept underground a lot of the time because there was nowhere else to sleep. You paid your 25 cents and got a bed. You had your own pillow. You had a piece of something to lay on, I guess. You carried a piece of blanket with you."

By February of 1945, he was wearing a corporal's stripes but lost them after a wild celebration — "an excellent time, a terrible time," he calls it — with his pilot brother Sam, who was returning to Canada. Side ended the war as a sergeant sending soldiers home or on to fight the Japanese.

Sam Side and his crew flew 40 bombing missions over Europe in RCAF 428 Squadron. P/O Side, second from the right in the back row, and F/Sgt Jack Naldrett, far right, were both from Dilke. The others were: back row from left, W/O G. Howard, bomb aimer and nose gunner, and W/O Allan Brownell, navigator. Front row from left, F/Sgt George Knight, RAF, wireless operator; F/Sgt John Bedford, RAF, flight engineer; and Sgt Stan Townsend, RAF, mid upper gunner. W/O Howard replaced F/O Patrick Murphy, who was a prisoner of war during the tour. Naldrett and Brownell married sisters and brought them back to Canada.

# IV.

# DILKE IN ENGLAND – THE AIR FORCE

MOST of them are long gone now, but during the Second World War Britain was dotted with air bases packed with men from many countries. Among them, spread from Sussex to Suffolk, Yorkshire and County Durham, were 19 men from Dilke serving in the RCAF or attached to the Royal Air Force. Six worked as ground crew, keeping the planes fit to fly. Five pilots, five gunners, a navigator, an air observer and a bomb aimer took to the air. Six men were killed: four in the deadly skies over Europe, one on a mission to Siam near the end of the war, one in a training accident over the North Sea in 1943.

Although airframe mechanic Art Boehme ended up in the Azores Islands in the Atlantic servicing RCAF aircraft on their way home in 1945, and even voted there in the federal election held that year, it was aero-engine mechanic Gus Koch who travelled farthest afield. Three experienced RCAF squadrons — 424, 425 and Koch's 420 — were moved to Tunisia in May of 1943 to fly their twin-engine Wellington bombers in support of the imminent landing in Sicily. They were based at Kairouan, about 35 miles inland from the Gulf of Hamamet.

"Life in North Africa miles from nowhere is just a nightmare of work and a terrific battle with the weather," Koch wrote to the Comfort Club on July 19. "Becoming slightly climatized we never refer to it being hot unless it is well over the 120-degree mark." For five days, he remembers, the temperature hit 125F. "Things were pretty tough one time, and I said there were two things I'll never complain about if I get

43

out of here alive. That's the food that's put on the table, and the weather. I've lived by that."

Koch had driven a big gas tanker from Algiers about 300 miles to the site — base may be too good a word for a place with no amenities for planes or men. With no runways, the bombers flew right off the ground to bomb Pantellaria (an island southeast of Sicily), Corsica, Sardinia and then Sicily before the invasion. The winter rains flooded the area, and when the water dried up the weeds were nearly three feet high. To make 'runways' for the planes, they mowed down the weeds with a motor blader. The men slept in tents, fought mosquitoes and ate tinned corned beef and hard tack. Their ration treats were two bottles of beer, two chocolate bars and 20 cigarettes every two weeks. On one 24-hour break from the constant work, Koch and two other men went north to the devastated city of Tunis, Tunisia's seaport capital — shelled by the army, shelled from the sea by destroyers, shelled by the air force; decimated.

Perhaps it was this desert service that led to Koch's mention in despatches, something he is still proud of today. The recommendation, dated July 22, 1944, said: "LAC Koch through his untiring efforts to fulfil his duties as a fitter has instilled a very high standard of efficiency and morale within his section. He is always cheerful under trying conditions, showing a true sense of loyalty towards performing his tasks in a faithful manner."

Koch couldn't wait to get back to England. After six months in Tunisia, 420 Squadron moved into a base at Tholthorpe in County Durham. In what was then and is now the high point of his war, he met his wife Heather in a nearby pub. An employee of the Ministry of Food, she was spending a week in the area picking potatoes, earning an extra week off for the demanding job. "This bright smile came up," she remembers of the night they met in a pub filled with air force personnel. One of only two women there, she chose Gus Koch and they were married the following year.

Reece Jones, too, found a wife during his air force service, with heavy bomber 431 Squadron based in Yorkshire and later at Tholthorpe. He was already married when he was sent in July of 1942 to Art Boehme's 419 Squadron to learn about the four-engine Canadian

Lancaster that was soon to be his responsibility. A year later, his wife Jean was posted to a station about four miles from his base and the couple lived in a nearby farmhouse. "It's really a great way to fight a war," he wrote to the Comfort Club. "After five o'clock, I can forget that I am even in the air force (and I like doing that little thing)." Living on the ration allowance was not all milk and honey, he admitted after receiving a parcel from Dilke. "One day you feast and the next you fast; you can imagine how welcome your parcel was to us because today happened to be one of the days we weren't feasting."

The passing of time can be traced through the men's letters. By July of 1943, when he met Jones in the mess at 419 Squadron, Art Boehme had been in England for a year and a half. He wrote home that Jones looked quite fit and well "but like most of us, the adventure of coming overseas has worn off." In 1944, as the Allies prepared to return to Europe and then went into action there, RCAF ground crews worked frantically to keep the planes in the air in support. All leaves were cancelled for several months, Boehme wrote in August, adding with quiet pride, "It looks as though our efforts were not in vain."

For his efforts, Boehme — who ended up a corporal — was mentioned in despatches in an award made on June 14, 1945. The commendation says: "This airman has always taken an extremely keen interest in all his undertakings. He has done an outstanding job at work in the capacity of an NCO and stands out among others in his untiring efforts to do all that he can in the interest of the service."

*    *    *

When he left the family farm at 20 to join the air force, Albert Horne had it in mind to be a gunner. A temporary problem with his eyes ended that ambition so, handy with machinery like all farmers, he opted for aero-engine mechanic. Part of 434 Squadron, based at Tholthorpe and then at Croft on the southern edge of County Durham, he was assigned to a specific Lancaster bomber. The work he and Jones (431 Squadron) were doing wasn't glamorous or glorious, he wrote in June of 1944. The glory "should all go to the boys who fly our kites." For the first year 434 Squadron did night bombing, but as the war began to wind down, it shifted to daytime raids. Ground crews' hours depended on how many flights were being made and how much maintenance was required when the planes returned. "We quit when our work is done," he said. He remembers aircraft coming back with holes in them, but fixing them wasn't his job. He had to keep the engines running smoothly and fill the aircraft with the fuel required for the next bombing raid. The squadron lost two or three planes in the early days. There was no great camaraderie between the people who flew the kites and those like Horne who kept them flying, he remembers. "I suppose if we had got to know our air crew better we would have felt more grief over it."

Aircraft were not congregated in one spot, where an enemy raid might wipe them out, but spread around to what were called dispersals, a cement pad joined to a runway that connected with the main runway. A hut on the dispersal sheltered the men when the aircraft was ready and they had nothing more to do. Not much of a one for pubs, Horne played quite a bit of blackjack of an evening, and remembers that he usually broke even. When he was stationed at Croft, near Darlington, he took dancing lessons in the city, but did not go to many dances. He was a shy farm boy, he says, though wartime rubbed off some of that shyness. So much so that he volunteered to serve in the Far East after the war ended in Europe, but Japan surrendered before he could embark.

Joe Ell's active war, on the other hand, was confined to six hectic months of flying, January to June of 1944. He wanted to be a pilot when he enlisted in July 1942 but when he heard that only the top people were taken to train on the touchy Link trainers, he opted for bomb aimer "because the bomb aimer is also the co-pilot in an emergency, and I liked that." The bomb aimer also photographed the bombing and its effect. "Everything was hooked up and you had all your sights up so that you looked along your sight, pressed your bomb finder switch, the bombs would come off in the order in which you had pre-selected them, and then at a certain time the camera would open. And then shut again. And then I'd say, 'That's steady, right, steady, bombs go out, bomb doors close, steady for camera, okay, picture taken.'" He laughs, remembering. "I don't know if I said that or not, but anyway, whatever I said."

A year of training in Canada was followed by more training in England, on two-engine Wellingtons and four-engine Sterlings and Lancasters, and he arrived at RAF 15 Squadron on New Year's Day, 1944. When they crewed up, he remembers, the pilot was Australian, he and the navigator were Canadian, and the two gunners, the wireless operator and the flight engineer were British; a Commonwealth group who became very close. They were based at Mildenhall, in Suffolk, a little east of Cambridge. He flew on 29 of the crew's 30 sorties, missing one through illness. Because one flight was to drop leaflets on France, it is not mentioned in the award of the Distinguished Flying Cross that was presented by King George VI. It reads:

"Flying Officer Ell has completed a successful tour of operations consisting of 28 sorties totalling 126 hours 40 minutes and including targets such as Frankfurt (2), Stuttgart (2), Aachen (2), Cologne and Essen. He has shown himself to be a skillful and accurate bomb aimer assisting his Captain to press home all attacks with precision and obtaining many successfully plotted photographs. In particular, on the night of 26th April 1944 he was detailed to attack a target in Essen and he secured an extremely good photograph in close proximity to the aiming point, although opposed by very heavy defences during the whole time he was in the target area. He is a most determined and gallant member of aircraft crew and his successes are an excellent testimony to the accuracy of his bombing." The citation says "completed … numerous operations against the enemy in the course of which [he has] invariably displayed the utmost fortitude, courage and devotion to duty."

Going to Buckingham Palace to receive the DFC is of course a highlight of Ell's years in the air force. The Australian pilot, Canadian navigator Art Cantrim and Ell received the honour, "even though the others went through the same dangers we did," he says, still puzzled. The day of the presentation he met Cantrim and his girl and they hired a taxi. "Art says to me, 'Joe, I'm going to say something I'll probably never say again' and when the taxi driver asked, 'Where to?', Art said, 'The palace.'" At the all-Canadian investiture, he remembers King George saying, "Mmm. When did you get this?"

When he finished his tour, Ell was stationed in Bournemouth on the Dorset coast, instructing. Then, as the Allies advanced and RCAF prisoners of war were being liberated, he worked in the wing involved in documenting the men, getting their paperwork done and shipping them home. Thereafter, he moved to a wing repatriating other troops who hadn't been prisoners. "And then I came home." If a person came through the war without injury, it was a great experience, he says. "But I hope there's not another war, because you know six of the boys in Dilke and district did not come back." He names the air force casualties off slowly: Dunajski, Reid, Church, Hills, Tait, Silverthorn.

"For years I didn't talk too much about it, because we used to refer to it as opening the hangar doors."

Alex Fuchs was another who didn't talk much about his air force service. He was the eldest of four brothers born on a farm northeast of Dilke. Frank joined the army and was killed shortly after D-Day, Tony chose the navy, and the youngest, Joseph, had received his call to service when the war ended. Alex Fuchs joined the air force in Regina on May 9, 1941, trained at various bases in Canada and reached England in February of 1942. He was a wireless air gunner serving with RAF 86 Squadron (Coastal Command) based at Gibraltar when his Liberator aircraft helped a Liberator of 311 (Czech) Squadron destroy a German blockade runner in the Bay of Biscay, on December 27, 1943. (The author is indebted to Hugh A. Halliday of Orleans, Ontario, author and historian who serves with the Canadian War Museum in Ottawa, for discovering this information.)

Fuchs and several others of his crew were awarded the Czech Medal for Valour early in 1948. He gave his family very little explanation about his trip to Ottawa in January that year to receive the medal, according to his brother Tony. But a nephew in Regina still has the medal with its inscription in Czech. Fuchs flew more than 558 hours with 86 Squadron, for a total of 31 sorties, and was based at various times in England, Northern Ireland and Iceland as well as Gibraltar, his brother says. He ended his air force career as an instructor, and was promoted to pilot officer in December 1944, shortly before he returned to Canada.

\*     \*     \*

Tom Koch was the eldest son of Joe and Margareta Koch, who were running Dilke's telephone office when the war broke out. He joined the RCAF before the end of 1940, followed within a few months by his brothers Gus and Frank. All three served overseas with the air force, Tom as a fighter pilot in 401 Squadron and Gus and Frank as Leading Aircraftmen with 420 and 415 squadrons respectively.

Tom Koch loved flying, and he wasn't eager to abandon his Spitfire when his first tour was about to end. "My operational time here has almost expired," he wrote home on February 22, 1944, "and I fear that I may be on rest when the great upheaval of the second front comes true, if it does. I would like to be in it, for then we will be in the midst of a real battle, instead of the comparative quiet operations we have been doing lately. It is not our fault, for the inactivity — we go forth, day after day, but the Hun will not come out to play, and most of the time we just dodge flak, and there isn't too much of it."

He predicted that soon there would be a turning point in the war, "and we will be called upon to do our utmost, and then we will make up for the dull operations we have been on." He got his wish to be part of that struggle. He was in the midst of his second tour, based in Europe, when he wrote again in November. The weather was not co-operating. "With a lot of rain and clouds, we have been unable to fly for three days. That makes me unhappy as I like to fly at least once a day, and if I don't fly it seems a day wasted! Not only is the day wasted, but I am certain the war is prolonged by two or more days." On December 18, when he wrote to acknowledge yet another Christmas parcel from Dilke's Comfort Club, the weather was still bad, but they looked for improvement. "We hope to collect a few scalps tomorrow, as the Jerries are up over their counter-attack and we want to get in on it."

Koch's 401 was the first RCAF fighter squadron, No. 1. It became 401 when all Commonwealth squadrons in Britain were renumbered to avoid confusion, and Canada got the numbers 400 to 450. 401 flew 12,087 sorties in the Second World War, and destroyed 195 enemy aircraft, plus 35 probables and 106 damaged. Six of its pilots were killed, 28 presumed dead, 18 taken prisoner and nine evaded capture.

Charles Ell of Dilke visited Koch at the squadron in 1943 and remembers the occasion vividly. Koch was called out during the visit on a sweep over France and asked Ell to wait. "He said, 'I'll be back in an hour.' I thought, Good God, be back in an hour. As soldiers, if we could say that ... if we got overseas it would be more than an hour before we got back. Anyway, I waited and I watched Tom take off with his flight and I was amazed, they were only six feet or so off the ground and they'd raise the wheels. The propeller would be just barely skimming the grass and they'd raise the wheels." Examining Koch's plane after the flight returned, Ell saw several holes. "They'd just gone over on a sweep over France and the anti-aircraft there had raked them."

New ideas were tested on Squadron 401, and Koch described two of those ideas in books published in 1995 and 1999 by Robert Bracken, *Spitfire: The Canadians* and *Spitfire II: The Canadians.* Articles in the books were written by former Spitfire pilots, and in the first volume, Tom Koch wrote about 401's adventures with Hotspur gliders. "Someone had the idea that when the invasion took place, fighters could tow gliders to France carrying ground crew and equipment," he explained. The squadron was based at Biggin Hill in Sussex, and Koch was one of three pilots who flew gliders on a test flight to Hutton Cranswick, with a lunch stop en route at Digby, on January 6, 1944. "Eyes must have been popping when we arrived at Digby and released our gliders from the towing Spitfires before landing." He carried the armament sergeant and parts for the tow hookup.

By February, Koch and others were training pilots of 411 and 412 squadrons on the gliders, and a brief training it was. "The first trip was a dual trip as the instructor pilot related the items to watch out for...On the second trip the pilot being trained flew the glider himself, with prompting by the instructor as required. The third trip was a solo. I can't imagine a shorter training period than that."

In all, Koch accumulated 175 minutes dual and 11 hours solo in gliders, and he loved being taken up high and released. "Then the slipstream noise became negligible and silence prevailed. I have imagined at times how wonderful it must be in a modern soaring flyer. In these, by taking advantage of up-currents, a pilot can be airborne for hours."

In *Spitfire II*, Koch described the dive-bomber missions the Spitfire was called on to perform, especially in 1944. "Thus, our aircraft in 401 squadron were equipped in 1944 to carry a 250-pound bomb under each wing, and a 500-pound bomb under the fuselage. Targets were 'no ball' (buzz bomb launchers), oil tanks, railway lines and bridges." He remembered leaving oil tanks blazing, hitting a railway line and perhaps delaying delivery of goods, and a good concentration on a bridge. What he found exciting was flying through the flak on the dive and when pulling up after the bombs were dropped. Not so successful was the experiment with a 1,000-pound bomb. One unhappy pilot — not Koch — had his Spitfire equipped with that load, and there was very little clearance above the runway when he taxied out, Koch wrote. The first two bombs released properly, but the third hung up and when the plane pulled out from the dive, the bomb pulled out part of the bottom of the fuselage.

"The aircraft returned to base alright, but much to our relief that put an end to the proposed 1,000-pound bomb on Spitfires."

*     *     *

For many Dilke people the war was a long and often boring, sometimes dangerous or deadly, interruption to their regular lives, but it brought Sam Side his future. Instead of returning to university in 1946, he took out a commercial pilot's licence and started a bush pilot business and flying school in Dawson Creek, British Columbia.

It almost didn't happen that way, however.

Knowing he lacked the military mind, Side chose the air force in 1942, figuring it would be less regimented than the army. No one noticed that he had asthma. When the recruiter listed the air crew positions, Side asked which was the best. 'Oh, pilot,' he was told. "Okay, I'll take that," he responded, with no idea what was involved. He says now he could not imagine himself a pilot and was sure he would not make it when he saw how many others failed, but "I just got into the routine, let things happen as they would." After a year of training in Western Canada, he went overseas early in 1943 and a year later joined a heavy bomber squadron, 428, based at Middleton St.

George in County Durham.

Before the men began operational training, the RCAF gathered them together in their various groups — pilots, navigators, gunners, etc. — in a big room and they had to form themselves into air crews. "Everyone took a look at each other, tried to read, and if a person was interested in flying with me, he'd come and ask if he could be my navigator or whatever the case might be," Side remembers. Out of the maze of people stepped Jack Naldrett of Dilke, Saskatchewan, determined to be rear gunner in a plane piloted by Sam Side of Dilke. Naldrett had had Perthe's Disease in childhood and spent two years in bed in a body cast; he was lame, Side says. "I don't know how he ever got into the air force." Side refused him flatly. "'No way, Jack, two of us from the small town of Dilke in one airplane, with all the losses.'" (Eight thousand, two hundred Canadians died in service to Bomber Command.) Naldrett insisted and eventually Side gave in, thinking "I'll ditch him somewhere along the way." They flew 40 successful missions together and Naldrett was a good rear gunner, "you couldn't have anyone better."

Side, the pilot, captained the aircraft, "even though the bomb aimer at the time had a commission and I was a lowly sergeant. I was responsible to them, and of course for them, if they did anything wrong. I had to make sure any appointments were kept, try to keep them as civil as possible. If any of them got in trouble, it was my duty to keep at them." But he was the one who got into trouble.

Before they took a plane over Europe, pilots had to do two trips with another crew for experience. Side's first trip was a harrowing initiation. He went to Berlin as second pilot to Squadron Leader Chris Bartlett from Fort Qu'Appelle, Saskatchewan, and found himself fighting fires after the plane was strafed by a fighter and hit by flak over the target. Bartlett managed to get the badly damaged bomber back to base. Shattered and unnerved after eight hours of exposure, and weighing the odds with survival as the prime objective, Side decided to opt out. "I decided there is no future in this. If this happens to an experienced crew, just think what's going to happen to me when I take an aircraft up." During the debriefing, he declared himself LMF, lack of moral fibre — absolute humiliation in the military, he says, de-ranking and relegation to the lowest of the low. He fell into bed about 7 a.m. and was awakened four hours later by an enthusiastic crew who told him there wouldn't be another familiarization trip and they were about to be briefed for a trip on their own that night.

"I told them I would not be going," he remembers, but he attended the briefing anyway, assuming the crew would be allotted to another pilot. "Somehow, still very tired and bewildered and seemingly by strategy of the powers that be, I ended up in the aircraft, reluctantly resigned to giving it one more try." They were sent with a full fuel and bomb load over the North and Baltic seas to East Prussia, feinted at Berlin and hit Magdeburg instead. Side remembers it as a frightful experience, especially in the target areas, but they managed to get back to base without incident, and his declaration of LMF was never again referred to.

Looking back, he thinks the RCAF had spent so much money on training him that they were hesitant to let him go. He was now a bomber pilot. He enjoyed flying, though he treated it as a job, "and truly that's what it was, just a job. I didn't know whether I wanted it to be my vocation." In October 1944, he completed his tour of operational duty and became an instructor. He was surprised to have survived. Airmen knew the odds against them — Canada lost more than 18,000 in the RCAF in the Second World War — and wouldn't even get their teeth fixed, he says.

Some of the danger came from the equipment. When he began his eight-month tour, four-engine Halifaxes were in use, but the version he flew was taken off major bombing missions. He flew 18 night missions in them to plant mines — 'gardening' — to tie up submarines and shipping in harbours, river estuaries and canals from northern Denmark to southern France, but finished his tour bombing major targets in a Canadian-built Lancaster. Both versions of the Halifax had design faults that made them hazardous and uncontrollable when certain evasive actions were taken, Side says. He agrees wholeheartedly with their description by author David Bercuson, in *Maple Leaf Against the Axis,* as killer aircraft, poorly assembled, cold, uncomfortable to fly and dangerous.

He remembers a run on March 3, 1943 to mine the Gironde River at

Bordeaux, France and pen the German submarines into their base. Planes had to go in low for accuracy because mines that fell on land might be found and identified as acoustic, magnetic or contact, and then they could be successfully swept. Mission completed, Side was climbing out when a crew member called, "Fighter attack, corkscrew starboard." Side reefed the plane over as he had been taught — drop the nose, turn into the approaching aircraft and dive. In the blackness, he had no idea how high they were above the Atlantic when the plane "went into a state of weightlessness, everything flew all over, it was just something to behold. But I managed to recover from it before we hit the water, and you wouldn't believe the shape of that aircraft after we recovered." Papers, maps, charts, codes flew off of every desk, batteries came loose, the Elsan chemical toilet in the rear — he can't bear to describe that. Side blames instrument lag. "When you do a sharp manoeuvre like that, there's a lag with instruments, it takes them a while to catch up to the position of the aircraft ... It's a normal procedure but what happened was the result of the design fault mentioned."

As the plane approached England from the south, the navigator was unable to pinpoint their location. The cathode ray tube, a sort of radar screen he depended upon, had been turned 90 degrees. "We come to the Bristol Channel, gee whiz, it was running north and south instead of east and west." The individual exhaust stubs on the engine began flying off and flames were enveloping the engine cowling, so Side landed at the first airport he saw, a RAF base in Cornwall. Although he had warned the ground crew not to remove the cowlings until someone came to repair the plane, they were removed and could not be replaced because they were warped, so the plane could not be flown. The crew, in battledress and flying boots, spent three days in the nearby pubs, knocking themselves out with powerful Cornish cider.

Side says the other problem RCAF bombers faced was being based in the north of England, the farthest north of all squadrons. They had to join the bomber stream near the Dutch coast, well within German night-fighter range. However, he says the pilots didn't have time to worry about the fighters, "the big thing was to get the load there and get back home." Pilots flying night missions preferred total darkness with no moon and/or overcast skies, but had to go with the limited navigation aids and weather forecasting of the time. Radio silence and unpredicted storms had to be accepted.

Looking back today, he believes the bombing was haphazard in its effectiveness. For example, on D-Day he took a load of bombs to drop ahead of the invasion forces. The target was fogged in and they had to take the bombs home, land with a full bomb load when the fog cleared a few hours later. He thinks the real value of the Allied bombing was the demands it made on German manpower and equipment. "They had searchlights and they had anti-aircraft and they had fighter pilots and everything goes to it. And besides that, the repair of the damage and everything else that was done, the injured and killed, the hospitalization. And their resources were very limited in terms of fuel and oil, and so that kept their aircraft up utilizing the precious fuel. That was, I think, the major effect of the bombing." It also kept the Russians happy that the West was doing its share… "regardless of the effectiveness."

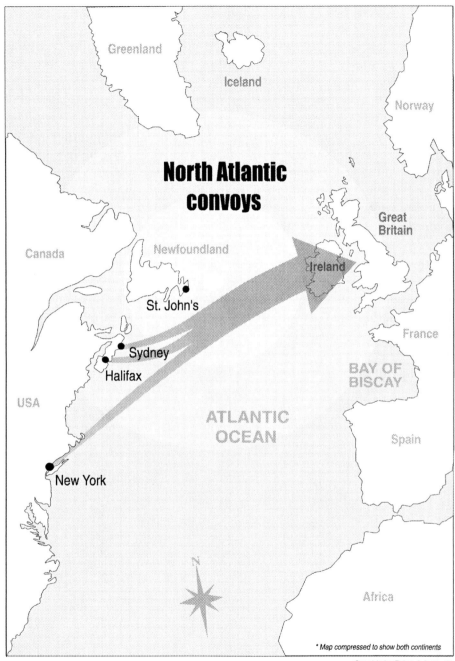

North Atlantic convoys

Greenland

Iceland

Norway

Canada

Newfoundland

Great Britain

Ireland

St. John's

France

Sydney

Halifax

BAY OF BISCAY

USA

ATLANTIC OCEAN

Spain

New York

N

Africa

* Map compressed to show both continents

*Graphic by Brian Johnsrude*

# V.

# DILKE IN THE NAVY

WHEN the Second World War began in 1939, Canada had a tiny navy. Joseph Schull's *Far Distant Ships: An Official Account of Canadian Naval Operations in World War II* — an indispensable source for this chapter — counted six fairly modern destroyers, five small minesweepers and two training vessels, with 145 officers and 1,675 men plus reserves. At the war's end, the fleet totalled nearly 400 ships plus hundreds of auxiliary craft, and nearly 90,000 men and 6,000 women in navy blue had done their nation proud. Among those were four Dilke men — Dave Amberson, Tony Fuchs, Bob Naldrett and Walter Wilton — surprisingly few in view of the numbers from the district who served in Canada's forces and the apparent affinity between prairie folk and the navy. There are no letters from any of them in the Comfort Club material, but Fuchs and Naldrett talked almost fondly in 2003 about their time in the navy. Amberson and Wilton died years ago without sharing much information about their service even with their families, though Amberson's sister Marg Doan remembers he was so young when he enlisted that their parents had to sign for him. He served on *Prince David*, Fuchs on *Magog* and *Waskesiu*, Wilton on *Sackville*. When Germany surrendered, Naldrett (nephew of the Bob Naldrett in the army's 8th Recce Regiment) had done his high seas training — he remembers he was the only one of 11 recruits who did not get sick — and he signed up on May 17, 1945 to go to the Pacific.

Tony Fuchs was the third of four boys born into a family that farmed north of Dilke and then moved to Regina in 1936, maintaining close Dilke connections that continue to this day. Since his older brothers Alex and Frank had joined the RCAF and the army, respectively, Tony opted for the navy when he was called up at 17½. He was almost 18 when he joined in Regina in November 1943 and began training on HMCS *Queen*, and then at *Cornwallis* in Nova Scotia. He says the navy wanted prairie people "because we didn't know anything (about the sea) and they could train us the way they wanted." Naldrett, who has a military tradition on both sides of his family and whose father Jack served in the Veterans Guard in Canada, enlisted in Regina in April 1944, age 18. Within a week he was on his way to *York* in Toronto for training, and then that summer to *Stadacona*, *Peregrine* and *Cornwallis* in Halifax until he did his high seas training on the destroyer *St. Francis* in April of 1945. He was actually a little disappointed when the war ended before "my first long tour" and he didn't get to see the world as the navy promised. "I was happy the war itself was ended, but I was kind of cut off short. It has always bothered me that I didn't get a chance to put in some long term on the high seas."

Fuchs was assigned to the frigate *Magog* based in Halifax and serving on convoy escort duty. But before following his adventures, we must build the historical framework through Schull's official history. When the war began, it quickly became apparent that trade between North America and Britain was as vulnerable as it was vital, and that the supply lifeline had to be protected from enemy ships and submarines. The British navy took control of British merchant ships, the Canadian navy of Canadian-registered ships, and would escort them in convoys across the Atlantic. The first convoy left from Halifax in September 1939. Schull eloquently describes that quiet beginning:

On September 16, one day after *St. Laurent* arrived from Vancouver, she moved outward through the Halifax approaches in company with her sister, *Saguenay*. Between the destroyers, waddling eastward with a certain untidy gallantry, were the eighteen merchant ships of Convoy HX-1 — Halifax to the United Kingdom.

Awaiting them in the open sea were the British cruisers *Berwick* and *York*, and beyond lay the sleety gloom of the Atlantic. The business of war had begun; and it was perhaps as well that the unaccustomed difficulties of convoy prevented too much speculation on the days ahead. (p. 17)

Until May of 1940, Canada's role was to shepherd the convoys from the coast to the high seas, where more powerful ships took over. Our navy was short of both ships and men. Prairie boys fresh from the farm sometimes had to be turned into sailors in three months. As for ships, Canada added to its tiny fleet first by purchasing three small luxury liners, *Prince Robert, Prince David* and *Prince Henry,* and converting them into armed merchant cruisers; the last two would shine on D-Day. At the same time, a new corvette was designed and built in Canada, and these "patrol vessels, whaler type" would play a huge role in the country's naval contribution and achievements during the war.

Perhaps the realities of that war really sank in for Canadians when the destroyers *Restigouche, Skeena, St. Laurent* and *Fraser* joined the desperate effort after Dunkirk to salvage a defeated British army from France. Then the first three of those ships joined in the critical battle to protect the southwestern approaches to Britain. Most of the rest of Canada's small but growing navy was helping maintain the long thin North Atlantic supply lines that kept that besieged Britain alive. Merchant ships were torpedoed everywhere. In the last week of February 1941, Schull reports, 150,700 tons of merchant shipping were sunk. In the first two weeks of March, 245,000 tons went down.

Late in 1940, the first of Canada's new corvettes moved down the St. Lawrence. In the mind's eye, we can see them steaming into the Gulf and the deadly seas ahead, bravely flaunting their oh-so-Canadian names — *Arrowhead, Arvida, Bittersweet, Chambly, Cobalt, Collingwood, Eyebright, Fennel, Hepatica, Levis, Mayflower, Orillia, Snowberry, Trillium.* Schull says they could travel at 16 knots and were armed with one four-inch gun, two machine guns and depth charges, but were untried, undermanned and sketchily equipped. They would soon have more men, more armament, more anti-submarine devices, more equipment of every sort. And they, and the dozens of sister ships that followed them down the river, would do Canada proud.

The first corvettes sailed into a desperate situation. By June of 1941, Schull reports, three merchant ships were sunk for every one replaced by Britain and the United States, while eight German submarines came into operation for every one sunk. There were U-boats around Britain and off Canada and the United States, U-boats in the Mediterranean, U-boats down near Cape Town, South Africa. And U-boats thick in the sea lanes where the convoys sailed. A new western defence system was developed, keyed on St. John's, Newfoundland, not then part of Canada. The first convoy leg would be the 500 miles from Halifax to the vicinity of St. John's, using local escorts which refuelled there and returned to Halifax. The second leg would use mid-ocean escorts from St. John's to Iceland, where the escorts would refuel and accompany convoys from Britain back to North America. On the final leg, British escorts would take the merchant vessels on to the United Kingdom. The organization of convoys was incredibly complicated, as Schull explains:

> Ship movements and cargo allotments had to be integrated on both sides of the Atlantic and around the world; and integrated again with war plans springing from the councils of Britain. Merchant ship movements, in convoy and out of convoy, were scheduled weeks and months ahead to insure that every precious bottom would be used to the best advantage. A ship's arrival for loading was co-ordinated with the arrival of trainloads of war supplies at a seaport and with the set dates for convoy assembly. Loading and assembly, again, were based on the requirement schedules of the United Kingdom. Each convoy as it moved to sea, a ragged agglomeration of weather-worn, rust-stained freighters, was in reality a cross-section of England's varied needs; a calendar from which the planning and progress of many vital operations might be deduced. (pp. 69-70)

In February of 1942, Canada's navy formed the main strength of the convoy escort forces in the western Atlantic, Schull says, with 13 destroyers and 70 corvettes. But the submarines still had their way. They sent 671,000 tons of shipping to the bottom just in June. In August, almost the entire Canadian navy was diverted to the defence of the Atlantic convoys, though it had to meet other calls, too. It responded to the Japanese threat in the northwest by sending *Prince Robert*, *Prince Henry* and *Prince David* — with young Dave Amberson of Dilke now among its seamen — and two corvettes to join the U.S. navy in escorting convoys in Alaskan waters.

The war was broadening in other directions, too, and Canada was asked to shift some ships to the proposed invasion of North Africa. They joined the great armadas targeting the ports of Algiers and Oran in Algeria and Casablanca in Morocco. In early November, six flotillas of Canadian landing craft put British and American troops ashore at Algiers and Oran, fairly easily since the Germans had been fooled about the objectives. But it soon became clear that success was not going to be easy in Tunisia and the long supply lines from Britain to Gibraltar and on into the Mediterranean had to be protected. In the constant warfare that followed, corvettes *Louisburg* and *Weyburn* were sunk, but by March 1943 the Allies had the upper hand. One by one the Canadian corvettes sailed back to Atlantic convoy duty where, in the worst weather of the war, at least 100 U-boats were on the attack.

In response, the convoy system was remodelled to involve aircraft carriers with a dozen planes that could search for submarines. As well, what Schull calls "the shore-based umbrella" was to be extended above the convoys. "From both sides intrepid crews operating at extreme range had been pushing out the radius of air cover; and their zones were expanding as larger planes came into service." (p.162) Soon the patrols by Canadian, British and American aircraft and crews would meet above the middle Atlantic.

Early in 1943, the Canadian navy took over from the U.S. all responsibility for trade convoys and their escorts north of New York to about 400 miles past Newfoundland. The U.S. retained control south of this area, and the Royal Navy to the east. The U-boat war had reached its peak. On March 9, five convoys were attacked at once. Seventy U-boats and 38 escorts were involved in the four greatest convoy battles that month; 37 merchant ships were lost. In all, 637,000 tons of shipping were sunk that March, Schull says.

Those must have been dark days for the Allied navies and the stalwart merchant ships they were trying to protect. But the dawn was coming. Italy surrendered, releasing ships from the Mediterranean. The new air-sea co-operation began to make an enormous difference to convoy security. By the end of the year, the long lines of communication across the Atlantic were safe. Schull delineates Canada's part in this success:

But the major Canadian contribution in the culminating year, as in all the earlier years, had been the ships of the escort groups. Sailing always with the convoys, herding the slow merchantmen onward through all weather, meeting danger and disaster as it came, their drab days were seldom brightened by the spectacular successes which fell to the lot of the hunting groups. Yet they had been the thin steel chain which had not snapped in the dark days, and they were the coiled mainspring of the offensive in the year of triumph. (pp. 182-183)

*     *     *

Canada was primarily responsible for the Atlantic convoys during the spring and summer of 1944, even as her navy was preparing for D-Day. Ships would carry the Allied armies to the beaches of Normandy, and maintain the lines of communication and supply connecting Britain and France. Nineteen Canadian corvettes were earmarked for invasion duties, convoying ships to the departure sites and guarding the assault lines from farther out at sea. *Prince Henry* and *Prince David* were converted to landing ships. *Prince Henry* was the senior landing ship in Force J, one of five assault forces, and on June 6 led 22 converted merchant vessels into position off the beaches of Juno sector; it also carried the eight assault craft of the 528th Canadian Flotilla and part of the assault units of the 7th Canadian Infantry Brigade. *Prince David,* the senior ship in one of Force J's subdivisions and the only ship there with a sailor from Dilke, carried the six assault craft of the 529th Flotilla and part of the assault units of the 8th Brigade. Out in front were 16 Canadian minesweepers, making the sea lanes safe for the ships that followed.

Seven miles from land, *Prince Henry* and *Prince David* and the rest of Force J lined themselves up before the Juno beaches. On board the troops prepared to hit the landing craft, and in their scheduled order, at their scheduled time, set off for France, a little over an hour away. Canadian destroyers *Algonquin* and *Sioux* fired at their targets on shore, two of 78 ships softening up the enemy. As the landing craft reached the beaches, the firing from behind halted. It was up to the soldiers now.

*Prince Henry* and *Prince David* returned early to Britain, leading their tattered landing ships and *Prince David* carrying 58 wounded soldiers. Not one Canadian sailor had been killed and only a few wounded, Schull reports. Ships now began carrying reinforcements for the relatively small forces which had gained a toehold in Europe, and supplies. *Prince Henry* led another group of landing ships on June 9 and made a third trip on June 18; *Prince David* sailed back on June 17. She would make two more trips in July, and *Prince Henry* three. They were still travelling through mined waters and could be attacked from sea and air, while the approach to the beaches was almost as risky as on D-Day.

In all, the two *Princes* carried 5,566 troops to Europe, and they did it well. "The accommodation and food provided for the troops had been, for the standards of war, superlatively good," Schull writes. "From commanding officers down, the men of the *Prince* ships were remembered, among far-scattered and diverse units now fighting ashore, for the good-natured helpfulness, the clean billets and the hot meals which had been the soldiers' unvarying portion during the tense voyages to France." (p. 326) The two ships were now re-assigned to the Mediterranean for an assault on the coast of southern France.

With their assault craft, they arrived in Naples on July 31. *Prince Henry* was designated headquarters ship for one of the subdivisions of the force, with an American naval staff on board to direct operations. She carried the First Special Service Force, a Canadian-American assault unit. Along with 283 French commandos, a British naval staff settled in on *Prince David*, headquarters ship for "Romeo" unit. The force moved off toward the Riviera on August 14, and by 8 p.m. *Prince David* and her entourage were in position 12 miles off Cap Nègre. They were to knock out its defences in preparation for commando landings at 1.30 a.m., landings which smoothly silenced the enemy gun positions and set commandos across the main road between Toulon and the coast. All the landings were successful, often lightly opposed, and by 4 p.m. the ships were sailing back to Corsica. Marseilles fell on August 23, Toulon on August 27. The operation was complete in two weeks and the Allies looked east to Greece, where *Prince David* would play a unique role.

On September 14, she sailed for the island of Kithera, between Crete and Greece's Peleponnesus, carrying 530 British commandos. The first wave went in anticipating trouble, but, Schull writes, was "greeted instead by crowds of rapturous Greeks, who not only warmed the hearts of the liberators with their welcome, but also fell to and assisted in the unloading of the craft." (p.365) *Prince David* was assigned to carry troops to liberate the island of Aegina, but it, too, had been evacuated. Canada's two *Princes* thereupon embarked on the expedition to liberate Athens. Seven landing ships preceded by three minesweeping flotillas and escorted by cruisers, aircraft carriers and smaller craft set off on August 15 for the port of Piraeus. *Prince David* carried Greek Prime Minister Georgios Papandreou and members of his government. As the first Allied ships sailed into the harbour, they were surrounded by small ships of every kind and greeted with tumultuous cheers from shore.

The vanguard of the expedition began to arrive on August 17. *Prince Henry* brought troops. *Prince David*, flying the Greek flag, transferred Prime Minister Papandreou and his party to a Greek ship, and on August 18 the Greek government returned to its liberated capital.

*     *     *

Back in Canada, *Magog* had been launched on September 23, 1942 and commissioned on May 7, 1944 at Montreal. She was assigned in August to escort and patrol duty in the vicinity of Halifax, Sydney and Gaspé. Tony Fuchs had joined her in April. "The first trip we made was to Bermuda for a practice run," he remembers. "It was so damn hot I got sick for five to six days." Their next trips were to Newfoundland and Labrador, where it was cold even in summer. Sometimes they were out 16 days at a time, he remembers, protecting ships on the first leg of the dangerous journey to Britain. They saw plenty of naval combat and dropped a lot of depth charges "but never saw a submarine" and never had to rescue any sailors from the water. He says he did not mind being in the navy, "but when you are used to the prairie, the ocean is not your thing." On the plus side, "we ate better than any of the armed forces did while we were at sea." He was at sea when the telegram came announcing the death of his brother Frank with the Regina Rifles, just three days after D-Day.

Fuchs served as one of about 20 lookouts per watch. He was usually on the bridge or in the prow near the guns, he says; only once for two dizzying hours was he in the crow's nest high above the deck. "You used binoculars and you just looked," watching for submarine periscopes. But nobody saw submarine *U 1223*, which sent a torpedo into the ship's stern on October 14 when *Magog* was one of the escorts taking a convoy of 60 ships through the Gulf of St. Lawrence. As usual, they were at the rear of the convoy that day, Fuchs remembers. He had come off duty at 8 or he would have been in the stern when the torpedo hit it about 10.30 a.m., blowing off the rear 60 feet, killing four men and wounding others. He grabbed his life jacket and ran on deck. "We never had a chance to fire back," he says. "There were a bunch of other warships there but they never saw it, though they dropped lots of depth charges." A seaplane picked up the wounded, and the ship was towed by a corvette the 200 miles to Quebec City. After less than three months on convoy duty, its sailing days were done. Fuchs remembers that the towing corvette was itself hit two days later, with loss of all lives. *Magog*'s crew spent about a month in Quebec City, "which I still say is the nicest city I've ever seen," and then were sent home on leave.

For the rest of the war, Fuchs served on the navy's first frigate, *Waskesiu*, which had sunk a German sub some months before he joined it. He had never smoked, but now did; after the torpedoing, "you were on edge all the time." On the *Waskesiu*, "we went from Halifax to Bermuda and trained, then three days in the Azores where we ate lots of fresh pineapple, then to Londonderry, Ireland for three weeks." The ship was at Londonderry when peace was declared. The night before, he remembers, "they made us all go to sea. We tied up in the Irish Sea with two British submarines." They returned to Halifax and then sailed through the Panama Canal to Vancouver, Victoria and Esquimalt. Fuchs was urged to re-enlist to serve in the Pacific, but he refused. He was just 21 when he returned to civilian life.

He enjoyed his time in the navy, he says. "When you're born on a farm you never see nothing." He saw a lot of ocean, including some southern waters where porpoises frollicked. There's not a lot of free time in the navy when your ship is at sea, he remembers, but a lot of men filled that time with gambling, especially after payday. "I'm not a very good poker player so I didn't gamble much," he says. Gambling filled in the three days on one trip back to Halifax when the ocean was so rough "they wouldn't let you stand lookout, wouldn't let you go outside." An experience he was happy to miss was the Murmansk run, with supply convoys to Russia. "It was all ice," he says. "One man on our ship had been to Murmansk and said they chopped ice every day."

\*   \*   \*

Even into 1945, with the land war progressing well and victory almost within the Allied grasp, the German submarines continued to take their toll on the convoys and their protectors. Canadian ships worked with the armies in mopping up port cities on the North Sea coast that had been bypassed by troops moving as fast as possible toward Germany. The Dilke men continued their service, while Bob Naldrett — finishing his training in Halifax — worried that he would miss his opportunity. Unless, like him, they had volunteered for the continuing war with Japan, they just wanted to get home fast.

Concluding *Far Distant Ships*, Joseph Schull sums up the Canadian navy's wartime achievements: 27 U-boats sunk alone or in company with other ships and planes, 42 enemy surface ships sunk, captured or destroyed. But the real story, he says, lies with the convoys:

> The statistics of battle are not unfavourable, yet they are the highlights struck off from a great and moving body and they are dwarfed by the main achievement. During 2,060 days of war, 25,343 merchant ship voyages carried 181,643,180 tons of cargo from North American ports to the United Kingdom under Canadian escort. Over the bridge which the navy helped to build and maintain some 90,000 tons of war supplies passed daily toward the battlefields of Europe.

Not without cost. We should know the names of the ships slain in our service, names that sing of Canada: *Fraser, Athabaskan, Regina, Alberni, Trentonian, Louisburg, Weyburn, Bras D'Or, Otter, Raccoon, Charlottetown, Chedabucto, Shawinigan, Clayoquot, Esquimalt, Margaree, Levis, Windflower, Spikenard, Ottawa, St. Croix, Valleyfield, Skeena, Guysborough* — and, of course, *Magog* — were the principal ones. In naval actions wherever war took them, 1,797

Canadians died, 319 were wounded, 95 became prisoners of war. In this count, at least, no men from Dilke figure.

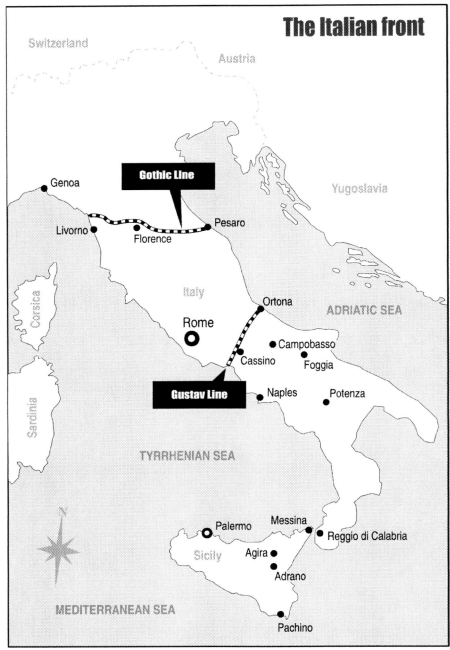

The Italian front

— Graphic by Brian Johnsrude

# VI.

## DILKE IN SICILY AND ITALY

IN 1943, the Allies determined to conquer Sicily, the football at the toe of Italy, and then invade mainland Europe through the Italian peninsula. Canada's 1st Infantry Division and 1st Army Tank Brigade sailed from Britain in late June to join the invasion armada as part of the British Eighth Army. Among them was Clarence Wray, a farm worker from Dilke who was a gunner in the fourth battery of the 2nd Light Anti-Aircraft Regiment, part of the 1st Division. He had been in the army for three years and in England since early 1941.

The Canadians arrived late on July 9 and 160,000 Allied troops began their amphibious assault on Sicily just after dawn the next morning. Canada's contingent went ashore near Pachino, close to the southern tip of the rugged island. Eighteen days later, after they had successfully fought their way northwest and then east toward the straits that led to the mainland, Wray wrote his first letter to the Comfort Club. It was July 28 — the day the Canadians dislodged the Germans from the mountain town of Agira, an important road junction, after five days of heavy fighting and many casualties. Not a mention of that hard-fought, costly success appears in Wray's letter, of course. Instead, he marvelled at Sicily, so hot, dry and dusty; perhaps it recalled Depression Saskatchewan. "Talk about getting brown in a hurry," he wrote. "I think we are nearly the same colour as the natives now." Despite the difficult mountain fighting, he had time to notice that Sicily's buildings were very small and its families very large. "Some of them live in caves. It sure is funny to see them crawling out of those holes in the ground."

He waxed eloquent about the excellent tomatoes and onions and the promise of fruit and nuts to come. "We managed to get three bags full of almonds last week," he said, from the 1942 crop. "I guess you would like to have some to put on top of a cake or just think of a nice Burnt Almond bar. Would like to have one myself." By August 15, he was camped in an orange grove with fruit ripe for the picking. Mouths must have watered back in Dilke at his report of pears, oranges, lemons, watermelon, figs, tomatoes, blue and white grapes, enjoyed in just one week. Ted Schultz with the engineers' 14th Field Company was no doubt enjoying the same delicacies, but he wrote no letters from Sicily.

They were soon joined by 20-year-old Steve Eberts, a gunner in 4th Reconnaissance Regiment, the Princess Louise Dragoon Guards. They went as reinforcements for the 1st Division, says Eberts. "When we got there, there were all sorts of ships in the harbor, sunk," he remembers. He had his first taste of battle while hastening by train to Canadian headquarters. "The engine was bombed on this train, and there we were in no man's land, in a grape orchard. We spent a couple of days there." He recalls high mountains, terrible, dusty roads and heat that put July in Saskatchewan in the shade. The PLDG won battle honours for their work at Adrano and the Troina Valley in eastern Sicily, as the 1st Division's armoured reconnaissance regiment. "Fighting all the way," Eberts says.

It took the Allies just 38 days to conquer Sicily and plan their move on Italy.

*   *   *

Envision Italy: a high-heeled boot stretching nearly 600 miles into the Mediterranean and riveted to the underbelly of Europe by a chain of rugged mountains. The Apennines are highest northeast of Rome, with peaks rising more than 9,000 feet, and lowest in the Calabria, at the boot's instep. At its widest point, the Italian peninsula is about 150 miles across, and river after river rises in the Apennines and runs into the Adriatic, to the northeast, or the Tyrrhenian and Ligurian seas to the west. Geography and weather join forces in Italy against an invader.

The Germans added a series of defensive lines: the Gustav Line, the most southerly and eastern, with the Hitler Line 12,000 yards behind it protecting the route to Rome; the Caesar Line stretched across the peninsula near its midpoint; the Bernhard or Winter Line on the Adriatic; and, most northerly, the Gothic Line, protecting the valley of the Po and the northern industrial region above the boot.

Ten men from Dilke were among the 92,757 Canadians who served in Italy. Three have already been introduced; they went to the mainland from Sicily. Soon to reach the battlefront from Britain are Lloyd Carr and Charles Reid in their tank regiments; Dean Amberson in his armoured recce regiment; Whitney Barry in an armoured car regiment; and artilleryman Harold Buck. The Royal Canadian Army Medical Corps will bring Mike Selinger, with a casualty clearing station, and Walter Scott, with No. 1 General Hospital, to help the wounded and ill.

Fresh from their Sicilian triumph, the Allies took the war to Italy on September 3. With the British, the Canadians crossed the narrow Strait of Messina to the Italian toe, while the U.S. Fifth Army landed farther north on the Gulf of Salerno, headed for Naples. Mussolini had been overthrown in July and the new government surrendered five days after the invasion. But the Germans immediately seized control, ensuring the war in Italy would be fought foot by slogging foot up the long peninsula. The Canadians landed unopposed and their target, the city of Reggio Calabria, was formally surrendered by Italian officers; the Germans had pulled back. After them went the Canadians, including Clarence Wray, Ted Schultz and Steve Eberts, who was driving a truck pulling the Dragoons' guns; the regiment had been turned into infantry and fought as part of the 12th Infantry Brigade.

Wray much preferred Italy to Sicily, he wrote on September 14 in one of his 25 letters to the Comfort Club. "It is not nearly so hot and this country is much cleaner. We have seen some wonderful things here." He was amazed and delighted at the women carrying items on their heads. "They carry buckets, baskets and clothes. I'm sure they must have some terrible spills when they are learning. Even the young girls carry things on their heads." The rural Italian washday attracted his attention, too. "There are lots of small streams and springs and that's where they do their washing. As the water is very soft, they use very little soap. Just rub them on rocks. And talk about snow white. You would hardly believe how clean they get them. And they don't have much trouble drying them as the sun is very strong."

He reported that some Italians watching his group eat were offered some of the tea that was going. They quickly rejected it as "no beauno which means no good." The Italians drink wine, he explained. "They grind them [the grapes] up stems and all, then they put them through a press and take the juice out. I guess it is about a year before it is any good." Italians certainly like macaroni, Wray said, "but ever since old Musso has had the upper hand, I guess he gave it all to the army. So they make homemade stuff and it's very good." The Canadians were enjoying new potatoes, green beans and corn on the cob. "We don't get those things in our rations," he was quick to add, "just gather them out of the fields."

Fighting their way north in a series of brief but bloody actions against the Germans, the Canadians took the mountain town of Campobasso, about a third of a way up the Italian leg, on October 14. They were in their battle dress rather than warm weather wear, Wray wrote, "and it sure feels good after the shorts. The only thing, it is very itchy. (No bugs). But I guess we will soon get used to it." At the end of that month, he painted a picture for the folks at home of how they lived in the cold and rain: "We have four blankets and an overcoat so we should be able to sleep warm enough. We also have small tents for two, and we have a large tarp that we fasten to the truck ... with poles and pegs. So we can keep out the wet. We have a radio receiving set and we get the news and some hot tunes."

Meanwhile, back in England, the Allies had decided to strengthen the Canadian forces in the Mediterranean. In November, the headquarters of 1st Canadian Corps arrived in Italy with, in stages, the 5th Armoured Division; five more men from Dilke entered the fray. Lloyd Carr was a crew commander with Lord Strathcona's Horse (Royal Canadians), the 2nd Armoured Regiment, which arrived in November. Charles Reid, a radio operator with the British Columbia Dragoons, the 9th Armoured Regiment, and Dean Amberson with the 3rd Armoured Reconnaissance Regiment, the Governor General's Horse Guards, came on December 19. The Strathconas and the Dragoons were part of the

5th Division's 5th Armoured Brigade; the Horse Guards were a key support unit. On January 5, 1994, Trooper Whitney Barry and the 1st Armoured Car Regiment, Royal Canadian Dragoons, arrived, attached to the 1st Infantry Division.

The families of Reid, Amberson and Barry had homesteaded in the Dilke area early in the century, but Carr came to the village with his mother and sister in the summer of 1940, shortly before he enlisted. The family were not strangers to Dilke, however; his father had worked there with the CPR and his mother had family there. So he counted as a local with the Comfort Club, but he never felt he knew the people who were writing and sending parcels and he is surprised today at the letters he wrote back. Like Charles Ell, he played the saxophone in army bands, but the instrument was left behind in England.

Carr had enlisted in the 16/22 Saskatchewan Horse, a cavalry unit transformed into a reconnaissance unit while he was training. In England, he was transferred into Lord Strathcona's Horse, which was short of trained personnel and wanted people with mechanical skills. He travelled to the Mediterranean in a convoy that was badly mauled before it reached Algiers, where he remembers doing a lot of marching as they waited in reserve for the Canadians fighting in Sicily. Dysentery hit them badly. "You'd see guys trying to go to the bathroom with no clothes on, all of a sudden they'd stop short, didn't dare try to move." Men lost their hair "from some sort of itching thing." Finally they shipped to Naples, and went into action.

In the early winter snows, the British Eighth Army, including Canada's troops, struck hard at the Sangro River on the Adriatic coast, hoping to relieve the pressure on the U.S. Fifth Army driving to take Rome. A series of deep river valleys cut the coastline; all were wild and swollen from tremendous rainfall. As Ted Schultz would later write home, "The geography of the country, the weather and the enemy are all against us, but we'll continue and eventually convince Jerry that 'Italy isn't really worth fighting for'." They pushed the Germans back from the Sangro. Charles Reid, radio operator in a British Columbia Dragoons tank, remembers what the infantry endured there, "in mud up to their knees and I guess they were fighting pretty near hand to hand." The Dragoons went to Italy without their tanks and equipment and took over Sherman tanks left by a regiment that had returned to Britain. The weather was terrible and the tanks got stuck again and again, "but I still think we had a snap compared to the infantry," Reid says. "At least when we were in the tank we could get our feet out of the mud for a little while."

Although Italy had impressed Clarence Wray after what he saw in Sicily, Reid — raised on a Saskatchewan farm developed over three decades — found it "a pretty backward place" where the farmers used oxen and donkeys. In the hot weather, he remembers, "you'd see the farmers go out with their oxen, early in the morning, at daylight, and they'd work till noon. I guess it was then they'd sleep."

*     *     *

As Steve Eberts noted, the Germans made their stands at the rivers, so when they were pushed back from the Sangro and their Bernhard Line was broken, they dug in on the Moro. On December 4, the Canadians were ordered to cross the Moro, where the tanks quickly bogged down in the river bottom. Five days later, they were across, with the medieval coastal city of Ortona their next target. It would take house-to-house fighting — at which the Canadians became the Allied experts — but Ortona fell on December 28. Lloyd Carr and the Lord Strathcona's Horse spent the winter there; he couldn't move his tank for the mud. He remembers they were under constant shelling, but the mud became their friend. "If one of the shells hit, it just went into the ground, way down deep in the mud, it just spouted mud up. You didn't get any blast from it." This artillery was not nearly so dangerous as when the regiment was in action, he found. He lived through this shelling in a slit trench with three other men.

On Christmas Night, Clarence Wray wrote to the Comfort Club, probably while smoking one of the cigarettes from the package that arrived that day. He happily reported that he was living in a house, "and it sure is good to be able to be away from the mud and dampness that you get when you are in tents." He had had a pretty good Christmas, he said. "We had a very good dinner today. Pork, potatoes, dressing, green peas and nice brown gravy. And for dessert we had pudding with sauce and mince pie. And tonight we had Christmas cake. We also had two bottles of beer and five chocolate bars. I think that is very good for soldiers on the move." With several musical instruments in the troop, "we had lots of music and some real singing." Outside, he said, the rain had made the roads and fields terribly muddy, but the weather was very mild for the time of year. "We can see the mountains from here and they are covered with snow now. It makes you feel cold just to look at them."

Mike Selinger was new to Italy and surprised, he wrote on February 1, 1944, at the quality of the Christmas dinner he had — roast turkey, Christmas pudding and all the trimmings. "The best part of it all was that while all ranks except officers and nursing sisters were seated behind white linen-covered tables, the officers and nursing sisters had the privilege of serving us in cafeteria style. They got a big kick out of it but to me it was a bang. We had a dance at nite which finished the day right. But they're not like the ones I used to know either. I'll be glad to go back to Canada and once again enjoy the peace and comforts of home and freedom." He could not imagine how the country around him had ever earned the name 'Sunny Italy'.

The Canadians were on the northern Adriatic front through January, February and March, much of the time patrolling the area north of Ortona. Clarence Wray was back in a tent, warmed by a stove made out of an old ammunition box with a stovepipe made from Italian rainpipe. Wood was hard to find, he said in mid-February, but they managed to get enough "to keep nice and warm" through the rain, wind and snow. "The Italians say the winter is nearly over," he reported hopefully. The regiment got five minutes of Canadian news on the radio each day. Steve Eberts slept the entire winter in a slit trench a few miles south of Ortona, always damp but never sick. His outfit was ferrying supplies up there, he says. "In mud clean up to the hips," Lloyd Carr wrote in early March, but lightened that bleak picture with the news that the grass was green, the olive trees were in full foliage and the flowers were starting to come through. "I am sitting just under an almond tree which is a mass of little white flowers. I had two almonds off this tree yesterday. They were from last fall's crop and hadn't fallen off." Whitney Barry of the 1st Armoured Car Regiment was hopeful. "We are now engaged

with the enemy, they seem to my notion to be taking quite a beating."
Happily, he reported on March 4, "the sun is drying up the mud so that
equipment can travel faster so I will be meeting you people before
long."

Artilleryman Harold Buck sent his first letter from Italy on March 10,
startled at what he was seeing. "I never dreamt that during a modern age
people could be so poor and backward. Money is not scarce, it is just
that there is nothing to buy. English houses are old and not the least bit
appealing but these here are absolutely repelling. Thank God we live in
a young country where there is acres of room and plenty of
opportunity." Perspective is everything. Clarence Wray had moved
from a tent into a large Italian house, and was delighted. "The room we
are in is very large and the ceiling is decorated with hand painting. I
guess some big shot must of lived here. Like all Italian buildings it
looks very shabby from the outside. It makes a very good place for us
to stay in. Nothing but the best for the Canucks." He also admired the
scenery. March 13 was sunny, after weeks of rain, snow and mud. "Sure
saw a lovely sight tonight. The mountains in the distan[ce] covered with
snow, and the sun setting behind them. The nights are very clear now.
It makes it much better for us when we do guard."

Lloyd Carr was in rest camp when he wrote to the Comfort Club on
April 29, "after eight weeks straight in the front lines." He was
expecting to be sent back there at any time. "Oh well," he wrote philo-
sophically, "the sooner we really get to it the sooner the job is over and
boy will that be the day."

*    *    *

The Canadians had little chance to appreciate spring on Italy's Adriatic
coast. In great secrecy, group by group, they had been moved south and
west for the next great battle, to break the Gustav Line and the Hitler
Line and move into the Liri Valley leading to Rome. The battle for the
Liri began on May 11 at the Gustav Line, which was breached four days
later. Steve Eberts remembers the town of Cassino, the linchpin of the
line, as being completely wrecked. He was driving an officer there one
day — the New Zealanders had replaced the Canadians in the line —

when a plane that had been shot down just missed his jeep. "We couldn't tell what kind of plane it was so we went over with our guns out, and it was a South African pilot. We helped him out and the plane blew up. That was a close shave."

Next, for Eberts and the Princess Louise Dragoon Guards, Carr and the Lord Strathcona's Horse, Reid and the B.C. Dragoons, was the Hitler Line. That battle opened up early on May 23, and by evening the line was breached across more than a mile. "We broke the Hitler Line," Reid says laconically. "A lot of that was British soldiers and so forth," Carr remembers. "We were in support of them. They got knocked off and when we went through them, we went into the Melfa River." After the line was broken, the 5th Armoured Division led the way to the little Melfa, which joins the Liri five miles to the northwest. The Governor-General's Horse Guards, with Trooper Dean Amberson in its ranks, went into action for the first time here, covering the flanks of the advance.

"The Melfa River was a pretty bad do at that particular time," Carr says. He explains that three tanks made up a troop, and when his unit went into the Melfa battle, the major of his group was in his tank. "We were pretty badly smashed up and this major took off and jumped out of the tank and left it. I was a senior NCO, a lance-sergeant, and I had to take over the command of the three tanks. They were damaged, tracks smashed... Of the three tanks we had, there was only my tank left." New men and tanks were sent up when they reached the Melfa, and they were so heavily bombarded from the mountains all around that the new troops and tanks were destroyed. Even today the memory of those raw troops dying all around him shakes Carr, but he says only, "It just got a little rough at times. You try to forget." In *The D-Day Dodgers*, Daniel G. Dancocks says the Strathconas destroyed 11 enemy tanks at the Melfa, and lost 17 Shermans and 55 men. Carr was wounded.

Still, both he and Reid say they felt safer in their tanks compared to the poor bloody infantry. "The only thing that would really bother us was heavy artillery of some kind," Carr says, "and certainly infantry didn't like tanks around them at all because they would draw fire. But in most instances, we were acting as artillery support for the ground troops so we were very close. In fact, quite often if we had to move fast, troops would climb onto the tanks and ride with us as we rushed ahead." Rushing ahead through olive groves brought its own problems. "The olives were falling off the trees and getting inside the tanks and you'd be slipping around." The smell soon made people sick.

By pushing the Germans north out of the Liri Valley, the Allies had opened the way to Rome. All five of the fighting regiments that included Dilke men — the Princess Louise Dragoon Guards (Eberts), Lord Strathcona's Horse (Carr), the British Columbia Dragoons (Reid), the Royal Canadian Dragoons (Whitney Barry), the Governor-General's Horse Guards (Dean Amberson) — won battle honours at the Liri. The Strathconas, the Dragoons, the GGHG and the PLDG also won honours at the Melfa Crossing, and the PLDG at the Hitler Line.

On May 31, the Canadians captured Frosinone and could see the plains stretching to Rome, but they were not to enter the city. It fell on June 4, to the Americans; the Canadians went into reserve. Things had been hot on the front, Lloyd Carr, now a lance-sergeant, wrote, "and we are on the move all the time, day and night, and have lost most of everything we had in the way of personal kit."

It would be a mistake, the Dilke veterans say, to think that any unit was constantly fighting. Most of the time they weren't in the front lines, Charles Reid says. "You go in for a spell, like I mentioned the fact that we went into the Hitler Line. Well, we went in and as soon as it was broken we came out." Rest and repair were the order of the day then. Clarence Wray wrote to the Comfort Club that on one leave he had been to a large city, with some very modern sections. "Also went to an opera while I was there," wrote this farmhand from Dilke. "It was very good. It was worth a lot just to see the opera house."

It was while he was doing reconnaissance near one of the many Italian rivers that Trooper Dean Amberson of the Governor General's Horse Guards was wounded. Harvey Doan of Regina, his brother-in-law, recalls Amberson describing how he was scouting ahead with another trooper when he saw a German sniper up in a tree aiming at his buddy. As he shouted a warning, another sniper in another tree shot into his left cheek, through his jawbone and into his right shoulder, where it cut some nerves. Amberson was shipped back to hospital in England, but he never again had full use of his right hand.

In July, the Canadians were moved north again, to the upper Volturno valley in central Italy to rest and reorganize for their next big challenge: the Gothic Line, which stretched across the peninsula from Pesaro on the Adriatic to near Massa on the west coast. In the hot weather, flies and ants were very bad, Clarence Wray reported from rest camp on July 1. Ants in your bed were particularly bad. But the rest period included lots of shows and ball games, very good sports meets and even swimming every day "if we feel like it. Some of the streams are as cold as ice as they come out of the mountains." After a visit by King George at the end of July, the Canadians were in place near Iesi on August 20. The main Gothic Line defences were behind the Foglia River, 10 miles to the northwest. The attack began on August 30, with the 5th Armoured Division playing a key role. The British Columbia Dragoons pushed 50 Shermans three miles through what was called Death Valley, "designed as a killing ground for tanks," says Dancocks in *The D-Day Dodgers* (p. 316). Only 18 tanks survived, but they broke the Gothic Line, Charles Reid says quietly, adding that the regiment lost its colonel (Colonel Fred Vokes, brother of Major-General Chris Vokes, commander of the 1st Division). The Shermans of Lord Strathcona's Horse took over from the Dragoons.

The regiments in which Reid, Carr, Eberts, Barry and Amberson served won battle honours at the Gothic Line, and at many of the battles that followed as the Canadians chased the Germans north; indeed, for their entire service in Italy. The men from Dilke rarely met, but they were fighting together in some of the heaviest sustained conflict the Canadians had experienced there. From the end of August until late October, they were in action almost continuously, with only brief breaks. Clarence Wray wrote home from hospital where he was convalescing from a wound, hoping to get back to his unit after six weeks away. October had the worst weather that anyone could remember. "Terrifically busy at the moment throwing 'it' back to Jerry, but not too busy to enjoy the box of Smiles 'n Chuckles received a week ago," Harold Buck, now a lieutenant, wrote to Dilke on October 1. "Fighting like mad at the moment in an attempt to get things cleared up before we have to spend another winter in this country. That would be a bit too much and break nearly everyone's heart."

The rain and the mud did their best to break people's hearts in that interminable time. Lloyd Carr, now a sergeant, wrote home on November 16 that it was no use telling about the weather because the news travelled faster than he could write it. "I can only say that when they say mud and rain has us tied up, the word mud is misused and they haven't found a word for this so-called Italian mud." On the brighter side, he had run into his cousin Clarence Wray several times, and found him not at all changed. Wray reported that the Italians were beginning to realize "they have been on the wrong side in this war. I must say it makes a big difference to the way they treat us." Steve Eberts remembers being stationed in a vinery in northern Italy, "with thousands of gallons of wine and vermouth" that they sampled. A dike separated them from the Germans. "I remember coming out of the area where we were holding the Germans on the other side of the dike. I filled up the jerry can with wine. Germans were shooting bullets in front of my feet" but he got the wine through safely.

Thanking the Comfort Club on December 10 for his Christmas parcel, Whitney Barry said the weather had improved "so it looks a little like sunny Italy instead of a steady drizzle of rain." What's more, "we are still going ahead slowly but surely. If it would stop raining and the sun shining every day we would be able to speed up our advance." Since it was too wet to pitch tents, they were quartered among "very nice" Italian people who welcomed them into their homes, he said. "We make signs and talk to them, they really think there is nobody like us Canadians. The senorittias *(sic)* wash clothes for us and sew and darn sox so we are very fortunate fellows. Of course there are some of these who give you a cold stare, we have them named fascists. There are quite often [partisans] here, they sure make short work of the fascists. We owe these partisans a lot of credit for their work in the fronts and ahead of the front lines, harassing the enemy to no end."

\*     \*     \*

It was now six months since the Allies had landed in France, and the eyes of the world were focused on northwestern Europe. The interminable struggle for Italy was almost forgotten. The battle for the Naviglio River that began on December 12 would be Canada's last full-scale effort there, and by December 20 the troops were dug in along the Senio, ready for Christmas. Clarence Wray visited Charles Reid. "He was the first one from home I've seen since arriving in this country although there are several [here]," Reid wrote to the Comfort Club on December 21. On January 2, the British Columbia Dragoons went into Sant' Alberto, their last hurrah in Italy. A month later, the entire Canadian contingent would begin its transfer to the Western Front, moving secretly out of the front lines and across the mountains to Livorno, or Leghorn. This was the first stage of Operation Goldflake, their move to Belgium. Men, 58,172 of them, and equipment, including tanks and other vehicles, sailed to Marseilles.

The 5th Armoured Division alone had to move 20,000 troops, including Carr and Reid, 5,600 wheeled vehicles, 450 tanks and 320 carriers. The first convoy left Leghorn on February 15. At Marseilles, remembers Reid, "they loaded us on a freight train, put the tanks on flat cars and we just stayed in the tank and rode along with them. These little old trains, they'd puff along and going up a grade they'd stall." Occasionally the train stopped and men ran to piles of wood which they carried to the engine. "That's what they were burning. No one had coal in Europe." Lloyd Carr remembers everyone's relief at being out of Italy. In this region untouched by war, the contrasts with the Italy they had seen so intimately were constant and striking.

Canada's tremendous effort in Italy has been pretty well forgotten by all except the veterans of that horrific 17 months. They don't forget how they kept the Germans fighting there, away from Normandy and D-Day, or that 55 German divisions had to be deployed in the Mediterranean in August 1944. Or that 5,764 Canadians were left behind in Italian graves, that 19,486 were wounded — including Dean Amberson, Whitney Barry, Lloyd Carr, Steve Eberts, Ted Schultz and Clarence Wray from Dilke, Saskatchewan, more than half the village's contingent in Italy — and 1,004 captured. It's not a happy memory.

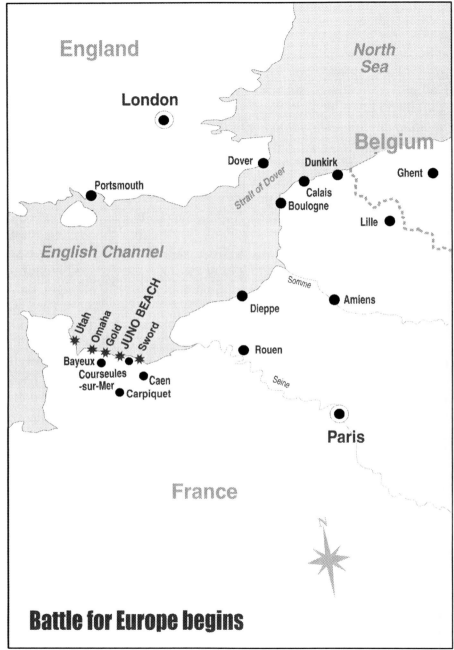

England

North Sea

London

Belgium

Dover

Straint of Dover

Dunkirk

Ghent

Portsmouth

Calais

Boulogne

Lille

English Channel

Somme

Amiens

Utah

Omaha

Gold

JUNO BEACH

Sword

Dieppe

Bayeux

Rouen

Courseules -sur-Mer

Caen

Seine

Carpiquet

Paris

France

**Battle for Europe begins**

# Chapter VII.

## DILKE IN EUROPE — D-DAY AND FRANCE

TODAY we know exactly what lay ahead of the hundreds of thousands of men gathered in Britain as 1943 turned into 1944, but they were in no doubt that the second front would soon be launched. "Rather looks as if the 'big push' is nearing the zero hour," Bob Naldrett wrote to Dilke on February 24, 1944, "and likelihood of our vacation in England coming to an abrupt end. Nearly three years for me now, so guess I can't kick." He had just returned to C Squadron, 8th Recce Regiment, as official gun fitter. "...Soon, I feel, there will be a turning point," fighter pilot Tom Koch wrote that same month, "and we will be called upon to do our utmost." They were optimistic. "Everything is just ready for the 2nd Front over here, all we are waiting for is the word Go," Fred Blancheon of the South Saskatchewan Regiment wrote on March 21. "I really have an idea Germany will fold up when it does open, let's hope so, we've been a Home Guard long enough." From RCAF 431 Squadron in Yorkshire, Reece Jones advised on April 28 that "the censors are bearing down on what we write to Canada which makes it hard to write...The old topic of weather takes a beating. It's really no small wonder it rains so much over here"; as if the rain responded to the need for something to write about.

The general D-Day story does not need to be retold here. Suffice to say that on June 6, 1944, the Allies landed in force on the coast of Normandy, which bristled with pillboxes, barbed wire, artillery, machine gun nests, mines, mortar pits and beach obstacles; the Germans' Atlantic Wall manned by battle-hardened troops. The Americans hit Omaha and Utah beaches to the west, while the British 2nd Army, which for the time included the 3rd Canadian Infantry Division, landed farther east on Gold, Juno and Sword. In *The Struggle for Europe*, Chester Wilmot described this area. The Canadians and British, he said, "were to land last, on the most exposed beaches, with the farthest to go, against what was potentially the greatest opposition. Because of the flow of the tide and the presence of rocks offshore, the 3rd Canadian and 3rd British Divisions could not begin to land until an hour and a half after dawn, during which time the enemy would have ample opportunity to prepare a welcome in a sector where his reserves were well placed to take advantage of any warning." (p. 273)

Canadian troops were carried to Normandy on Force J, led — as we saw in Chapter V — by Canada's *Prince Henry,* with *Prince David* heading a subdivision. They were just two among 109 Canadian ships in the 7,000-strong Allied armada. No doubt it's impossible, but how fine it would have been if Dave Amberson of Dilke, serving on *Prince David*, had been able to wish good luck to Frank Fuchs, Ed Brandon, Stuart Laing and Ernest Burns of Dilke before they landed with the Regina Rifles, the Royal Winnipeg Rifles, the artillery's 13th Field Regiment and the 4th Armoured Brigade of the Royal Canadian Army Service Corps, respectively. They were in the 7th Infantry Brigade which, with the 8th Infantry and 2nd Armoured Brigades, assaulted Juno Beach in the British centre. We will follow the 7th with its Dilke men, but it also included the 1st Canadian Scottish and the 1st Hussars (6th Armoured Regiment), supported by the Royal Canadian Engineers and the 14th Field Regiment.

The Canadians were to establish their bridgehead and then push through the gap between Bayeux and Caen to Carpiquet airport 11 miles inland. After a mighty bombardment, the 7th Brigade landed to the right on a five-mile sector of Juno Beach called 'Mike'. A Canadian Scottish company and some Royal Winnipeg Rifles made it ashore without much trouble, for naval gunfire had shut down the German battery on their beach, the right flank. On the far left, the Regina Rifles, with Frank Fuchs, touched down just after 8 a.m., and had good support from the tanks of the 1st Hussars as they moved ahead. But between them, B and D companies of the Royal Winnipeg Rifles came under heavy fire from enemy strongholds that had survived the bombardment. In a few hours, the two companies lost almost three-quarters of their men, but still they cleared the minefields and moved into the nearby villages. By 9 a.m. their reserve units, A and C Companies, were landing, and Rifleman Ed Brandon of Dilke reached France again, two years after his brief visit to Dieppe with the South Saskatchewan Regiment. The Winnipegs fought towards Banville, silencing several pockets of enemy resistance that had been bypassed. C and D Companies took the village.

By noon the 9th Brigade had moved ashore from its reserve position and was trying to exploit the gains made by the 7th and 8th. By mid-afternoon, a 1st Hussar troop had crossed the Caen-Bayeux road, the farthest point achieved by the Allies on June 6, but was forced to pull back because it had pushed ahead of the supporting infantry. By the end of the day, the Allies had landed about 155,000 troops in France, plus vehicles and matériel. The Atlantic Wall had been breached, at the cost of about 10,000 killed, wounded and missing. The Veterans Affairs Canada website reports that 340 Canadians were killed, 574 wounded and 47 taken prisoner. Compare that to the toll at Dieppe almost two years before: 907 dead, 2,460 wounded, 1,946 captured.

The Germans counterattacked in the early hours of June 7, through the gap that still separated the Canadians on Juno from the British on Sword Beach, but the invading force held firm. Together, the Regina Rifles and Royal Winnipeg Rifles then advanced on their final D-Day objective — the Caen-Bayeux road and railway near Putot-en-Bessin. They share the glory of being the first Allied units to reach their goals, and consolidated their position at Putot. Both regiments earned battle honours for their achievements in the Normandy landing.

On June 7, the invasion forces linked up and moved steadily inland, approaching Caen and Bayeux. Now began the second part of the Allied plan: the German strength, particularly its armoured strength, was to be drawn onto the British-Canadian front while the American armies broke out on the western flank and swept south and then east to the Seine. It worked; the British and Canadians were able to pin down seven

German panzer divisions on the Caen front for almost two months, taking heavy casualties. On June 8, the forward companies of the Royal Winnipeg Rifles were cut to pieces but the Canadian Scottish later retook the lost ground at heavy cost. The Regina Rifles' front line was overrun, their headquarters area infiltrated, in a desperate all-night battle. On June 9, Frank Fuchs of Dilke — just old enough to vote — was killed by a sniper; Ernest Burns saw his body that day, he told Fuchs' family after the war.

Also representing Dilke in France by now were Pete Thauberger with the engineers' 3rd Field Survey Company and Jerome Gartner in the Ordnance Corps. Unfortunately, none of the Dilke men who reached Europe in June was as prolific a letter writer as Clarence Wray, whose details about Sicily and Italy added so much to the previous chapter, and no one ever referred in a letter to the landing. But on June 26, Stuart Laing wrote from the 44th Battery of the 13th Field Regiment, RCA, to acknowledge his latest parcel from the Comfort Club, especially the cookies. "It was a real treat to taste such rich food again. We have just been getting tinned rations so far and there is not much variety among them so it does not take very long to tire of them." He was wishing he'd paid more attention to French when he was in school. "A French-Canuck is made right at home. In fact, we all are, but we have that disadvantage." On July 5, Rifleman Jerome Gartner of the Ordnance Corps sent thanks for a parcel and the farm weekly, *The Western Producer*. When he next wrote, on August 5, Gartner would be with 1st Canadian Scottish Regiment, which had to be re-manned after its heavy losses; his lieutenant was Ed Schwandt from Strasbourg, Saskatchewan, who taught school in Dilke before he enlisted and was the first secretary of the Comfort Club. Schwandt would be dead before summer ended.

Since D-Day, Allied ships had been constantly conveying troops to the French beaches, and other Dilke men were eager to get into the action. "It's been pretty noisy around here since the 2nd front opened only three days ago," Butch Side wrote on June 9. "So far have not been privileged as being one of the boys in it, but some day a chance will come, very soon I hope." Side never got this chance. "I suppose you were all excited about D-Day," Walter Tate wrote on June 18. "Myself,

I was rather disappointed! Still we will all have our chance sooner or later." His chance came very soon and he was wounded by July 18. Jack Mangel was bitter that he was not in France with the 27th Armoured Regiment (Sherbrooke Fusiliers), reporting that he had been moved to a holding unit and his category lowered. "So they may send me home before the war is over. I'd just as soon stay here though. I can do more here than I could back home." Presciently, he predicted at least another six months of war in Europe, but thought Japan would not last long once Germany was finished. "Our boys seem to be doing alright in this second front. How I wish I could be right in there with them. I always wanted to see action. But I haven't got a chance in the world now."

Others from Dilke were almost as deeply into the second front as the men on the spot. From the ground crew of RCAF 420 Squadron at Tholthorpe, County Durham, aero-engine mechanic Gus Koch wrote on June 30, three weeks after receiving a parcel from the Comfort Club: "I am sorry I haven't written sooner but you will understand and realize we have been terribly busy this past month. This is no ploy, we mean business. Many a time I haven't seen my bed for 48 hrs but I don't mind in the least as it has to be done, the sooner the better."

*     *     *

As July opened, thousands more Canadians were readying in England to cross the Channel with the 2nd Infantry Division and join the fray. With the Division's reconnaissance arm, 8th Recce Regiment (14th Canadian Hussars), on July 4 came four Dilke men: brothers Lloyd and Lawrence Smith in A Squadron, Bob Naldrett and Bert Tait in C Squadron. Three days later, the rest of the Division landed, including in its 6th Brigade the South Saskatchewan Regiment and the Queen's Own Cameron Highlanders of Canada; Fred Blancheon and Leo Selinger returned to France nearly two years after their bitter experience at Dieppe. Alan Wilton and Walter Tate and the artillery's 2nd Anti-Tank Regiment also reached French soil. Fourteen men from Dilke were now in France, one of them already buried near Courseules-sur-Mer.

On July 8, 8th Recce Regiment went into action for the first time at Carpiquet airport to relieve the 8th Brigade, which had been in the line almost constantly since D-Day. Lloyd Smith, a gunner operator on a four-man armoured car, had a Besa machine gun and a 37-mm gun, peashooters compared to the Germans' big 88s, as he would soon find out. He remembers his first encounter with the enemy. They had driven all day to reach Carpiquet airport and "here were these guys, Jerries, laying dead. We were out walking around and here a goddamned Jerry airplane came around and started shooting us. There was a guy with an armoured car and he had a machine gun to get the aircraft and we shot him down. That was our first look at things." After the airport was taken, "we were having tea and we look out the window and here are the Jerries coming right at us ... As soon as they saw us they went back. I just got on the radio and phoned the troop headquarters and they sent me up and we got 20 prisoners that day. And after that everything broke loose and we were gone." They drove all night and reached Carpiquet Sunday morning; the town was taken that day.

It took a month to capture Caen, a city of 55,000, but it finally fell on July 9 to 2nd British Division and 3rd Canadian; the Regina Rifles, the Royal Winnipeg Rifles and 8th Recce won battle honours. On July 18, Walter Tate sent a Priority Casualty Postcard to his mother in Dilke, telling her he had been wounded with the 18th Anti-Tank Battery, 2nd Anti-Tank Regiment, but was going on well and hoped to soon be out of hospital. The next day, Fred Blancheon wrote the Comfort Club, grateful for a box of 300 cigarettes since the daily allotment was just seven, plus a chocolate bar and some sweets. He had been wounded on his first trip to France on August 19, 1942, but this time he was able to look around with a farmer's eye. It was "not a bad country but has been knocked about a bit, and it will likely be worse by the time everything is done," he said. "The French are not so bad, they treat us well. I guess the Canadian flag has flown beside the French flag quite a few times lately." Rain was needed to settle the dust.

Leo Selinger of the Queen's Own Cameron Highlanders wrote on August 6 not quite from the front, "but what you may call the next thing to it which is not out of range by a long shot." He painted a realistic picture of life as a foot soldier. "A fellow really has to keep low with all the bombs and shells flying over your head and around you. I've been in some pretty tight spots and managed to get out alive so I hope the future will not be so bad." He thought things had been going along pretty well, but he had learned one thing. "I never figured mother earth was so dear to me until I came to France. I used to curse when I was being told to dig a trench but now they have to tell me to get out of it. Just the same, it's a great war..." He found France more like the open fields of Canada than England had been, and the climate dry with many flies and mosquitos. All in all, "a pretty nice country and would be a lot nicer if it hadn't been for all the holes in the walls or nothing left to the buildings except a mass of ruins."

On August 7, 1st Canadian Army launched a massive night surprise attack from Caen toward Falaise 20 miles away, the home centuries before of William the Conqueror. A thousand tanks and armoured vehicles with mounted infantry moved off in Operation Totalize, which involved the 2nd Infantry Division, the 2nd Armoured Brigade and 8th Recce Regiment in the bloodiest fight yet of the Normandy campaign. They headed into a land of softly rising ridges strongly held by the Germans, Brigadier-General Denis Whitaker, Sheila Whitaker and Terry Copp wrote in *Victory at Falaise,* with the farming villages between the ridges turned into fortresses. "The battle from Caen to Falaise was a bitter two-week drive ridge by bloody ridge, mile by grudging mile, across the rolling cornfields of the Caen plain," they wrote (p. 183). As the tanks consolidated to beat off any counterattacks, the 6th Brigade and the Scottish 152nd followed, clearing out the villages passed by the armour. Snipers held Roquancourt for six hours against the South Saskatchewan Regiment, and the Queen's Own Cameron Highlanders had a stiff fight at Fontenay. But by noon on August 8, Canadians were six to seven miles deep into enemy lines.

Lloyd Smith of 8th Recce's A Squadron had his fateful meeting with the German 88 on the road to Falaise. "There we were sitting with a great big 88 looking right at us and the crew commander said, 'Get ready to shoot.' What the hell am I going to do with a little popgun? A Besa machine gun and a 37-mm, that's all we had. I never even got a chance to shoot it. That shell ... when they pulled the trigger on that thing, that shell was there." Smith's driver, who sat below him in the armoured car, was killed; Smith and his crew commander were wounded. "I don't know where that shell even went," he says, still marvelling at its speed. A 77-mm was the nearest they had to this 88 "and you could count 10 before it landed. That 88 was there as soon as it went off. Oh, man, the velocity." That was the end of his combat experience, but the effects are with him yet. "I know I could have lost my arm," he says casually, "but it don't bother me at all." Except that it is always cold.

He remembers a mined region that focused the tanks into a certain area "and the Jerries were hid underneath the ground and once we passed over then they came up. So we said nothing like that and then they postponed it for two weeks and they bombed the heck out of it. After that they [the Canadians] broke through and away they went." But it was too late for Smith. He had been sent back to England to hospital and reached home in November, to be hospitalized in the Department of Veterans Affairs ward in Regina. His crew commander was sent back into action.

During a lull in the action, Pete Thauberger wrote to friends in Dilke that while the troops weren't yet permitted to buy anything in France, he had sampled French wine and found it just to his taste. Ernie Burns — 'Happy' to his hometown — wrote to the Comfort Club on August 14 from a foxhole where he was happily sharing his latest parcel with four men who had missed supper. "I'm doing fine here in France," he said nonchalantly. "It is warm but dusty, but I have seen some dust in my day, or should I bring that up?"

The next day, the 6th Brigade was ordered to take Falaise immediately. The South Saskatchewan Regiment was pinned down at the town gates, but the Queen's Own Cameron Highlanders forced their way in, supported by the tanks of the Sherbrooke Fusiliers, the 27th Armoured Regiment that had left a bitter Jack Mangel in England. On a boiling hot August 18, Falaise was cleared of Germans; thousands surrendered. All the regiments with Dilke men won battle honours there or on the bloody road leading to the town: the SSR, Camerons, 8th Recce, the Royal Winnipeg Rifles.

\*   \*   \*

In *The Long Left Flank*, his detailed examination of Canadians' action from August 1944 to the war's end, Jeffery Williams describes the Canadian Army's position as August drew to a close.

> 1st Canadian Army was always to advance northward from the beachhead to cross the Seine between Rouen and Le Havre. Having closed the Falaise Gap and beaten off the enemy's desperate efforts to break out of the trap, General Harry Crerar was to begin one of the most arduous campaigns of the war — unsung because unspectacular, seen as "mopping-up" — but some of the bloodiest infantry battles of the war. (p.18)

For three days in late August the Canadians fought with German troops covering their army's withdrawal across the Seine at Rouen, on the north bank. Late on August 28, the enemy armour was across and the infantry moving after it. The Canadians followed — popular Dilke teacher Ed Schwandt was killed crossing the Seine — and were welcomed into Rouen on August 30 by cheering civilians. Their next job, writes Williams, was "to take Le Havre, secure Dieppe and destroy all the enemy forces in the coastal belt up to Bruges," in Belgium.

Imagine a right-angled triangle in northwestern France with its right angle dug into Rouen. The base of the triangle will stretch left, or west, 50 miles to Le Havre on the coast. Go straight up from Rouen for about 35 miles and you reach Dieppe, the top of the triangle. On September 1, that's what the Canadian army did, two years and a bit after its first tragic visit. No one expected it to be easy. As it marched north on August 31, the 2nd Division was led by its eyes and ears, 8th Recce Regiment. Behind came the regiments that had raided Dieppe, each with its veterans of that terrible August 19: the South Saskatchewan and the Queen's Own Cameron Highlanders with Fred Blancheon and Leo Selinger of Dilke, the Essex Scottish, the Royal Regiment of Canada, the Royal Hamilton Light Infantry. They were expecting a fight and, indeed, they had a sharp encounter with a German anti-aircraft unit withdrawing from the Le Havre peninsula, and another at Langueville. But by nightfall, 8th Recce, with Lawrence Smith, Bob Naldrett and Bert Tait of Dilke, was almost at Dieppe; the rest of the division trailed behind it for 10 miles or more.

"We went to take Dieppe but when we got there, no Germans," was how Fred Blancheon — wounded there two years before, one of Dilke's first wartime casualties — described the Canadians' return for the folks back home, in a letter written a month after the day of triumph. "They knew we were out for revenge and pulled out rather than face us."

The 8th Recce battle history says its squadrons competed to be first to enter Dieppe the morning of September 1, and A Squadron won, making Lawrence Smith of Dilke one of the first Canadians to return to the coastal town whose name is engraved on the nation's heart. At 10.30 a.m., Canada entered a Dieppe filled not with Germans but with crowds of French civilians delirious with joy at their liberation, offering flowers, wine, kisses and embraces. There was time for the veterans of the raid to visit the battlefields they had fought on and the cemetery where their dead comrades lay. Two days later, the entire 2nd Division marched proudly through Dieppe in columns six abreast, to another tumultuous welcome. General Harry Crerar, commander of 1st Canadian Army, was there to take the salute on this day so vital to his country, though the history books relate that General Bernard Montgomery was furious with him for missing a conference and let Crerar know it when he did show up.

The Canadians could not stay in Dieppe to be feted, of course. 1st Canadian Army had been ordered to clear the coast and open the Channel ports to receive vital supplies for the Allied armies, clearing the approaches to Antwerp, the second largest port in Europe. This part of Canada's army had two corps, 1st British and 2nd Canadian. The British were to clear out the Le Havre peninsula and take the city. The Canadian Corps, comprised of 2nd and 3rd Canadian Infantry Divisions, 4th Canadian and 1st Polish Armoured Divisions, had its work cut out for it on the French coast and on into Belgium. The 2nd Division was to move nearly 100 miles north and east and begin clearing the whole coastal area east of Calais, including heavily fortified Dunkirk. (It would eventually be decided to contain Dunkirk with minimum forces and move on to the more important task of opening Antwerp.) The 3rd Division was charged with taking Boulogne and its 10,000-strong garrison, 25 miles before Calais. On September 3, the Corps crossed the Somme, led by the Polish Armoured Division, and drove northward. The Polish armour crossed the border into Belgium on September 6 and overcame enemy resistance at Ypres and Passchendaele, names that resonate from the First World War. It then moved into the Ghent area, halfway to Brussels, the capital. The 4th Armoured Division also moved into Belgium. We will find them all there in the next chapter.

During September, some of 1st Canadian Army's divisions were transferred to Operation Market Garden, a bold but ultimately unsuccessful scheme to cross the Rhine and win the war. The 2nd Division was ordered to Antwerp, so the 3rd, with the D-Day veterans, had the formidable task of taking Boulogne on its own. The battle began on September 17 when waves of Lancasters and Halifaxes dropped 3,000 tons of bombs on the defenders, and the city surrendered after five days of stiff fighting. Meanwhile, the 7th Brigade, with Dilke men in the Royal Winnipeg Rifles and 1st Canadian Scottish, had been assigned to capture Calais and Cap Gris Nez while Boulogne was besieged. It quickly proved too much for one brigade, and the attack on Calais was put off to September 25, when all three 3rd Division brigades plus artillery and aircraft laid into the city. The Canadian Scottish fought their way to the coast while the Royal Winnipeg Rifles captured the 18th-century stone fortress of Fort Nieulay. After a truce to evacuate civilians, the Queen's Own Rifles attacked Calais from the north, the Regina Rifles from the south and the Canadian Scottish from the coast and captured the city. All these regiments proudly list Calais in their battle honours.

Canada had a wonderful name in France, Blancheon wrote on October 3, "and we have adopted Caen, as that was where Hitler lost the war. He really took a beating there. We had our share of it too, but he got the worst end." Back in England, he said with longing, his new wife "has a lovely home ready for me for when I get back, so you can guess how eager I am to get home." He ventured a bold prediction. "We should have the war over with by the end of this month, at least we are hoping so. It has been nearly five years since I left Dilke." He would not return permanently to England for more than a year.

Others were there, in hospital. Leo Selinger of the Queen's Own Cameron Highlanders was recuperating in 24 Canadian General

Hospital and then in Roman Wall Convalescent Hospital from a serious wound that stretched from one foot up his leg to mid-thigh, lifelong memento of a German grenade. He wrote to the Comfort Club in early December that he had moved to the convalescent hospital for physiotherapy "so as to be out of the line of being a cripple." Lloyd Smith of 8th Recce Regiment left England for Canada in November, and spent time in hospital in Regina.

Behind them, Canada's war was shifting to Belgium.

# Chapter VIII.

# Dilke in Europe — Belgium and Holland

OUR Dilke men had little time for letter writing that fall of 1944 as the Canadian Army finished clearing France's Channel ports and faced off with the Germans in Belgium. Further south and east, the Americans and British were pushing directly toward Germany. As the Canadians occupied Ostende on September 9, as they felt out the enemy along the canal connecting the historic cities of Ghent and Bruges, the Allied leaders were looking beyond to Antwerp. Though the enemy still had troops in and around the city, the British had captured its huge docks virtually intact on September 4, but they could not be used. Even at October 1, the Allies could land supplies and matériel at only three ports: Dieppe, its subsidiary Le Tréport and Ostende. Antwerp, larger and much more convenient as the fighting shifted toward Holland and Germany, had to be opened up, and that job was handed to 1st Canadian Army.

Even a modern map of the region shows why it was such a challenge. Antwerp is almost 60 miles inland and linked to the North Sea by a winding estuary, the West Scheldt, much of which runs through the Netherlands. South of the estuary is flat polder country — land at or below sea level that has been rescued from the sea and enclosed by dikes. North is the Dutch province of Zeeland, now a peninsula shaped somewhat like an arrowhead pointing into the sea. A marvellous map in Jeffery Williams' *The Long Left Flank* (pp.84-85) shows that in

1944, it was more like three islands, with the easternmost tied to the mainland by an isthmus five miles wide at its widest point and pierced there by the Beveland Canal linking the Scheldt's west and east branches. Then the land widened into South Beveland, with the smaller North Beveland island to the north. Reaching deepest into the North Sea was saucer-shaped Walcheren Island, with one long, thin connection to South Beveland. This was the Germans' Fortress Scheldt, an invader's nightmare of dikes, water and guns that had to be taken to open Antwerp to supply ships.

Here's how the Canadians were to free the Scheldt and make the docks at Antwerp usable:

- Clear the area to the north and close the South Beveland isthmus.
- Clear the Breskens "pocket" behind the Leopold Canal, in the polder country south of the estuary.
- Take the Beveland peninsula.
- Finally, capture Walcheren Island.

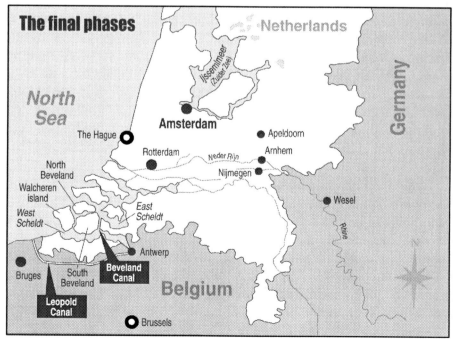

—— Graphic by Brian Johnsrude

It would be just over two months from the time the Antwerp docks were freed on September 4 until Walcheren Island was in Allied hands. The Battle of the Scheldt would last from October 1 to November 8, and cost 1st Canadian Army more than 12,000 casualties, including 6,367 Canadians. The Royal Winnipeg Rifles, the Regina Rifles, 8th Reconnaissance Regiment and the Queen's Own Cameron Highlanders — all with Dilke men — would dearly earn the battle honours they won there.

As October opened, the 2nd Division (with seven men from Dilke) was advancing north and east of Antwerp toward the South Beveland isthmus while the 3rd Division (with three Dilke men) and the 4th Armour began an assault over the Leopold Canal, nearer the coast. All fought through flooded terrain, claiming yard after bitter yard from determined defenders who took a heavy toll. The 6th Brigade, with the South Saskatchewan Regiment (Fred Blancheon) and the Queen's Own Cameron Highlanders of Canada (Leo Selinger), tried twice to get across the Antwerp-Turnhout Canal northeast of Antwerp and twice failed. When they finally got over, they headed west toward the isthmus while the 4th Amoured Division was closing in on it from the north. The entrance was sealed off on October 24, breaking the land link to Fortress Scheldt.

On October 26, Fred Blancheon told the Comfort Club his latest parcel was "a real treat especially after what we have been eating lately." He gave an update on the war: "We seem to be still plugging away at old Jerry, but every day is one day closer to the end of the war. We have the doodlebugs to contend with, they are plentiful too. The Army has broken its heart and has promised us 48 hrs every six months," he said sardonically. "Isn't that a wonderful thing to look forward to." He really liked Belgium and its people, he said, adding, "I don't think things are going so well in Holland for us, too much German." It was nearly four years since Blancheon had left Canada, and it shows. "Well, folks, I guess we'll be home some year, I hope it's not very long."

They weren't grumblers, these Dilke men. In *The Long Left Flank*, Williams describes the conditions they were enduring, but did not mention.

The abiding memory is grey skies, rain, fog, bone-chilling dampness, boats, battledress and blankets soaking wet, cold food, matches that wouldn't light, the soldier's weariness that is as much fear as lack of sleep, and everywhere, mud and water. (p. 115)

On the southern shore of the Scheldt, the 3rd Division was fighting fiercely to cross the 90-foot-wide Leopold Canal and clear the Breskens pocket. The Germans held every possible crossing place on the canal, but the Canadian Scottish and one Regina Rifles company carved out a narrow bridgehead on October 6 and defended it tenaciously. For five days the Reginas were pinned to the bank, "some 10 yards from the enemy," Williams writes. An amphibious assault broke the enemy hold on October 9 and the bridgehead was enlarged; tanks could now cross. By November 3 the south shore of the Scheldt was free.

Operation Vitality, the strange name for the battle for South Beveland, began on October 27. The 6th Brigade attacked toward the formidable Beveland Canal, while the South Saskatchewan and the Camerons were to grab the road and rail bridges and locks. It was dawn, light enough to see that the bridges had been blown and the enemy held the far bank. The SSR scrambled across the broken bridges to grab a foothold and held it amid bitter fighting while a bridge was thrown across behind them. 8th Recce Regiment, with its three Dilke men, was working westward along the north coast with members of the Dutch Resistance. By October 29, it was apparent that South Beveland would soon be clear and troops were preparing to attack Walcheren Island, the last obstacle to Allied use of the port of Antwerp. This final stage was called Operation Infatuate. (Where did these names come from?!)

The only link between South Beveland and Walcheren Island was a long narrow causeway that carried a road, a railway, a bicycle path and a thin line of poplars. The Allies decided the strongly-defended island should be attacked from the east across this causeway, from the south across the Scheldt, and from the sea. First, it would be bombed heavily to breach its enormous dikes and let in the North Sea so amphibian craft could be used. "By the end of October," Jeffery Williams writes, "the island resembled a saucer filled with water." (p. 148) On the rim of that saucer were the German coastal defence batteries, some big enough to engage a battleship. The assault began early on November 1 with artillery fire, followed by a naval battle with the main German batteries in which every Allied ship was hit, and then commandos landed at several spots. The weary 5th Brigade was ordered to take the causeway, which quickly became 'the road of death'. The brigade took enormous casualties but managed to dig out a small bridgehead before it was relieved and sent out for a week's rest while the steady progress continued. Walcheren Island was Canada's show, but it involved British infantry and commandos as well as 2nd Canadian Division. The last Germans surrendered on November 10.

Two days earlier, Bob Naldrett wrote to Dilke with gratitude for a parcel of food "as canteens and tuck shops are more or less a thing of the past." He was weary of bully beef, canned vegetables and hard tack, but noted that he'd seen lots of good beef lying around dead. "I counted 18 head all in a bunch one day, but we are generally too busy when we first see it, and [it's] too high for our Canadian palates if we should run on to it a week or so later." He was writing while 8th Recce enjoyed a brief rest period behind the lines — "or they call it a rest period, but we really have more work to do than when in action, getting arms, vehicles, etc. in shape for return to action." As C Squadron's official gun fitter, "my job is checking the large calibre guns and this is the only time I have a chance to do it thoroughly." He had so far managed to steer clear of trouble in action, he said. "My closest call was from one of our own men, who jabbed (accidentally) a bayonet in my cheek one hectic night when we were on guard and expecting a visit from Jerry, a young chap and the strain made him nervous." There speaks the calm veteran of nearly four years in the army. "Luckily it didn't penetrate too far and the scar is hardly noticeable now."

The capture of Walcheren Island ended Canada's bloody battle of the Scheldt. By November 26 the approaches to Antwerp had been swept free of mines, and two days later the first supply convoy arrived. Leading the 18 ships, appropriately enough, was the Canadian-built freighter *Fort Cataraqui*, with a British crew.

Fred Blancheon was a lance-corporal in the South Saskatchewan Regiment when he wrote to Dilke 10 days later, on December 6. For the first time, he referred to the weather, "a bad stroke of luck, otherwise this war would be over. The rain has put a stop to the fast moving we were doing. We only had three fine days in November, so you can imagine the state of things here." But he was eternally optimistic. "Still if we could only get a few weeks now of good weather we could drive him clean out of Germany. I think this is going to end just like a snap of your fingers as any morning I would not be a bit surprised it was over."

He knew that Canadians at home had been told that their troops were getting leave in the big cities, and felt it important to set the record straight. "We are not getting any leaves so if you read in the papers about us going to Paris, Bruxelles, Ghent and Antwerp, just think of a few, and I mean a few. They are giving a few a 48 hrs to those cities. If the war lasts till 1948 I expect I'll have mine by then if the zombies don't get priority." Despite that bitterness, he was optimistic that things "are going in our favour, but too slow for me. I like to move every day then I feel like we are winning. Anyway, we'll be home for next Xmas or you will know the reason why."

*     *     *

Now began a winter among Holland's dikes, quagmires and rivers, and our men from Saskatchewan's recent dustbowl must have marvelled that a land could hold so much water. "Here in Holland we find the climate very damp," Pete Thauberger wrote dryly on November 27, "but are in high hopes of giving it the 'final touch' in Germany soon and then back to good old Canada." After months of constant fighting, they weren't exactly enjoyed a rest period. The job of 1st Canadian Army was offensive operations between the river Maas, deep in Holland and very close to the German border, and the Rhine. The Canadian front ran from close to the German frontier more than 200 miles to Dunkirk, on France's North Sea coast.

The battle history of 8th Recce Regiment says it relieved a brigade from the 3rd British Division on the Maas and spent the balance of the winter there, near Nijmegen. C Squadron was in the centre at Beugen. In a letter written as 1944 came to a close, Bob Naldrett doesn't of course name the place, just says the squadron was stationed in an evacuated village a little too close to the enemy and patrols came by regularly to a pretty warm reception. "He's a tricky beggar," Naldrett wrote, "and seems to have an endless supply of chaps who can speak English equally as well as we. Not near as many now as he used to have, though." The frozen ground was "much preferable to the rain, mud and slush we had the first few weeks we were in Holland." They were billeted in houses, most of them with furniture, and had a good supply of coal so were quite comfortable. "We even had electric lights for some time but the power came from Germany, but guess he got 'hep' to the score and turned it off."

At Christmas they had enjoyed "one of the best dinners I have had since I have been in the army: turkey, dressing, spuds, brussel sprouts, plum pudding, sauce, bread, butter and tea. No liquor, but this is hardly the place for that." He had received the Comfort Club's Christmas parcel in good time. "I too had hoped you had sent me, at least, my last Xmas one, but if Jerry insists on taking a worse beating than he already has, we are the guys who can give it to him, and I mean by 'we' the Canadians."

Jerome Gartner was stationed in a large Belgian city, "not at all smashed or damaged like some of the cities in France," he wrote on January 1, 1945 after an enjoyable Christmas and New Year's Eve. "These people are great," he said. "They call us 'Liberators' and certainly treat us good." After his brief stint with 1st Canadian Scottish Regiment, he was serving as an interpreter – his German was fluent but he also handled Dutch and Flemish – with the Army's No. 2 Base Reinforcement Group, which settled in Ghent from October 1944 until the end of the war, according to a report written for the Army's Historical Section and available on the Internet. Stuart Laing, Dilke's representative in the artillery's 13th Field Regiment, met Gartner in Ghent when Laing was on a 48-hour leave, "but he was in a hurry so we didn't have much time to chat," he told the Comfort Club in a letter written December 7, 1944.

Ghent was special to Laing's unit, he told the folks at home. "You see, the whole unit had been there about a month ago and we made some very good friends. We lived with civilians, two of us in each home, and they treated us wonderfully. When I came back, I was fairly swamped with letters different people had written to fellows in this battery." As for the war, "we are in a very static position now," he said, "just holding but not giving Jerry any peace." They were on the lookout for some turkeys "that might make a good Xmas dinner." He was grateful for the socks in his Christmas parcel, for socks were about as scarce as turkeys.

As 1944 turned into 1945, our Dilke men must have known that the war was nearing its final days, but their letters reflect more war weariness and stolid determination to see it through than anything else. "Things are pretty much the same over here, but every day is closer to the finish," Fred Blancheon wrote on February 1, 1945. "We hope it won't be long now though, all I hope is Stalin has good brakes so that he can stop when he meets us." Ahead lay the offensive to drive the Germans back over the Rhine to final defeat, and the liberation of the great cities of the Netherlands, Amsterdam, Rotterdam and The Hague, suffering through the "Hunger Winter." Joining in these efforts would be the Canadians who had fought so long and bravely in Italy, linked up just before the war's end with friends and comrades they had left behind in England more than a year before. How much had changed!

\*    \*    \*

In February 1945, the Allies launched their first great offensive into Germany with two sets of thrusting pincers: 1st Canadian Army would advance from the Nijmegen area southeast to clear the German lands between the Rhine and the Maas, and the U.S. Ninth Army would push northeast against the rear of the armies opposing the Canadians. They were to meet on the Rhine opposite Wesel. The Canadians of the 2nd and 3rd Divisions — now including eight men from Dilke — had three huge tasks before the Rhine: to clear the Reichswald Forest, break the mighty Siegfried Line and clear the Hochwald Forest.

In *The Long Left Flank*, Jeffery Williams describes what lay ahead in this offensive into the Rhineland:

> Lying across its western approaches, a barrier of mountains and a great river form the historic natural defences of the Reich. Buttressed by them, inside its borders, lay the 'West Wall', built by Hitler before the war.

From the Swiss frontier to the northern border of Belgium, in places three miles deep, a defensive zone of mutually supporting fortifications, anti-tank obstacles, minefields, wire, protected command posts and troop shelters blocked the Allied advance. In 1944, the Siegfried Line, as it was known in the West, had been extended northward along the Dutch frontier. (p.181)

Through constant patrols and careful observation, the Canadians had learned all they could about the enemy forces ahead of them. Operation Veritable was launched on February 8, after an enormous air and artillery attack, with seven infantry and three armoured divisions and three independent armoured brigades, plus artillery with more than 1,200 guns. Mud and flood made progress difficult, especially for armour. When it was possible and helpful, the infantry rode in amphibious vehicles. On they slogged, taking the outer defences of the Siegfried Line, and then foot by foot pushed through the pine forests of the Reichswald and the water-logged countryside beyond until, after two horrendous weeks, they cracked the mighty defence line. Fred Blancheon of the South Saskatchewan Regiment cut the vaunted Siegfried Line down to size in a letter written March 7 from hospital where an infection in his arm was being treated. "I was on the Siegfried line when I had to come out. I really expected to see some wonderful defence positions, but it was not as big as I thought it was. Seen much bigger, when we came through from the coast."

"Well, I've finally set foot on the sacred soil of the Fatherland," Stuart Laing wrote on February 14, just eight months after he landed on D-Day with the 13th Field Regiment of the Royal Canadian Artillery. "Quite an achievement, we all think, but I sure wish I could see the country under different circumstances. There's nothing left of the towns but a big pile of rubble. The end looks very close now, so we might get home for the opening shindig in the hall I hear there is talk of building." (He certainly did get home in time, for Dilke Memorial Hall, named in honour of the local men and women who served with the armed forces, held its grand opening dance on June 4, 1948.)

Next would come Canada's Operation Blockbuster, launched on February 26 against the Schlieffen Position and involving three Canadian divisions and two British divisions under General Crerar. The job was tougher because the U.S. Ninth Army was held up by stiff fighting and so the Canadians faced "the best German troops on the Western Front and backed by a mass of artillery," Jeffery Williams writes in *The Long Left Flank* (p. 221). By the end of the day, and despite the loss of more than 100 tanks and 1,000 casualties, the Canadians had the momentum. The next day they began their drive into the Hochwald area, another state forest. Again they faced boggy farmland defended yard by yard by a determined enemy backed by an incredible weight of artillery. The battle history of 8th Recce Regiment refers to "terrible roads, A/Tk guns as thick as flies." But by nightfall on March 4, the area was cleared. The Americans too were on the move, breaking through the fanatical resistance, and on March 10 the Germans blew up the bridges of the Wesel and abandoned the land west of the Rhine. 1st Canadian Army had fought grimly through impossible terrain and weather to crucial success. It lost 15,634 killed, wounded or missing, including 5,304 Canadians, but was sitting on the bank of the Rhine. The Rhine, the Rhineland, the Reichswald, the Hochwald — they fly proudly in the battle honours of all the regiments in the 2nd and 3rd Divisions in which Dilke men served.

*    *    *

Even before the Rhineland offensive began, the Allies were planning the liberation of Holland, and gave the job to 1st Canadian Army. The campaign would bring together all the Canadian troops in Europe, because the veterans of the Italian campaign — 1st Canadian Corps — had at last reached the front in North-West Europe. Now nearly two dozen men from Dilke were representing their Saskatchewan village in the dying days of the war with Germany. "Though the move was long and tiresome we enjoyed it very much," Clarence Wray wrote on March 28 from the 2nd Light Anti-Aircraft Regiment in Holland. The local people "are very good to us," he added. "Just make us feel as if we were home." "We are at present billeted in the homes of some very sociable Belgium families," Harold Buck of the 11th Field Regiment wrote on March 20. "All we are waiting for now is to get in on that 'one big push' that Churchill spoke about. And if Montgomery's words of last

Sunday are true then it won't take long after we join shoulders for that push." Steve Eberts had moved to the Regina Rifles, "and I've met a lot of the boys from the district," he wrote to Dilke on June 27.

The story of the liberation of a hungry and desperate Holland echoes with names like Emmerich, Apeldoorn, Zutphen, Deventer, Groningen and Arnhem. Ed Brandon and the Royal Winnipeg Rifles were involved in the 7th Brigade's capture of Zutphen, cheered on by the residents. On April 6, the Brigade began the successful attack on Deventer, where those of the enemy who weren't killed or captured tried to flee, "across the Ijssel through a curtain of fire laid down by guns of the 1st Canadian Division, being heard for the first time in North-West Europe," writes Jeffery Williams in *The Long Left Flank* (p. 265). Both the Lord Strathcona's Horse (Lloyd Carr) and the British Columbia Dragoons (Charles Reid) earned battle honours at the Ijsselmeer. Carr remembers a bridge near Nijmegen. "We had quite a scrap over that before we were able to get across it. Infantry saved it, but we were some of the first troops to cross over the bridge and advance on from there." He also remembers their tanks travelling under grape vines and being smeared with smelly, slippery grapes inside and out. "You'd have to clean them up, you couldn't live with it." Lester Duesing of Dilke, newly come to Holland with the 1st Division engineers, had just one battle in his short wartime career, struggling to put a floating bridge across a Dutch river. The assault on Arnhem began on April 12, and the town was cleared after two days of house-to-house fighting. Late on April 16, the 4th, 5th and 6th Brigades, including Fred Blancheon and the South Saskatchewan Regiment, took Groningen.

"We just went into action in the Netherlands for just a short period of time, kind of a cleanup," Charles Reid of the British Columbia Dragoons recalls in his understated way about 1st Canadian Corps' liberation of western Holland. Then the Canadians turning to feeding the starving Dutch; after the war, says Jeffery Williams, "it was estimated that mass starvation had been avoided by only a matter of two or three weeks." (p. 290) This was the end of the war for 1st Canadian Corps, which spent the remaining time before the German surrender guarding the Grebbe Line.

However, 2nd Canadian Corps was still hard at it. The 5th Armoured

Division was clearing the final corner of northeast Holland, and the 2nd, 3rd, 4th and Polish Divisions were capturing the Emden-Wilhemshaven promontory north of Bremen, in Germany. They were having great success against a disheartened, overwhelmed, frightened enemy when they learned that the war at last was over. On May 5, Canada's General Foulkes accepted the surrender of the German troops in Holland and General Simonds did the same on his section of the front. The formal German surrender came on May 7.

North-West Europe sits proudly among the battle honours of all the regiments in which Dilke was represented.

# Chapter IX.

# DILKE IN EUROPE — GERMANY

THE war in Europe was over, and in regiments scattered around the liberated continent, battle-weary men from Dilke and every other Canadian hometown thought only of getting across the Atlantic as quickly as possible. "We look forward to one thing now and that is our homes," Lloyd Carr told the Comfort Club exactly a week after Germany surrendered. "There is yet work to do but our homecoming isn't very far off." From Belgium, Harold Buck wrote pessimistically on May 28: "All of us here are anxiously waiting our turn to get home though some of us will probably just make it in time for that Christmas turkey. At any rate, we are certainly looking forward to getting back on the home soil which we love so much."

Getting back would be considerably delayed for a lot of Canadians, however. Immediately after Germany surrendered, 2nd Canadian Corps was temporarily occupying part of the prostrate country while 1st Corps units moved into Holland's major cities. Fred Blancheon wrote on May 27 from the South Saskatchewan Regiment with his first thoughts on Germany. "This is really a lovely country, wonderful farming land and nice homes. You can see they have lived off the fat of the land. The female population are very pretty, far more than the male; they seem brutal looking, domineering." Then he corrected himself. "I should say still there are some pretty tough looking females." He was resigned to staying in Germany a while longer. "Well, we have this end of the war over. Now we have to occupy the land for some time. Sure wish I was out of the army now but there is nothing to do but wait." Clarence Wray was in Holland, in a small town near Groningen. Writing on June 3, he reported that the crops were growing well, "a good thing as food is very scarce." Canadian troops would help gather the harvest. Later, two months after they had stopped fighting, he wrote, "There are rumours that we will be going back to England soon. But will believe it when we get there." Among many other things, the army had taught these Dilke men realism.

As the months passed with no immediate prospect of getting home, boredom set in. "At the moment we are leading rather a dull life while waiting to move off to England and then home," Harold Buck wrote on July 11 from his artillery unit. "When I say dull I mean there is no work to do but all the opportunity and facilities in the world to enjoy sports and other recreations. You might think it strange that such a life should be called dull — but believe me it is. By all means give us the same opportunities at home where the loved ones are and I would tell you all was heavenly."

His words bring to life statements in Report No. 174, "The Canadian Army Occupation Force in Germany, May 1945 to June 1946," prepared by Major C.E. Brissette of the Historical Section, Canadian Military Headquarters and available on the Internet. It says, in paragraph 50, "...the transition from fighting to occupational duties brought with it new problems for our troops. They had more leisure time on their hands. And mentally they were not keyed up to the pitch of the days of intense action. To fill in much of this spare time, new measures were soon introduced which urged all ranks to take advantage of the various courses provided by the army through educational services. All forms of sports were organized within the units of the division and sports meets took place on a division level. Auxiliary Services provided a wide range of entertainment which included moving pictures and stage shows." The efforts were appreciated. "I saw a swell show in town, put on by the Canadian Army Entertainers," Walter Tate wrote on July 5. "They come here quite often, so with the cinemas, etc., we do not lack for entertainment." He had returned to Europe with RCAF 666 Squadron, run jointly by the air force and army, "holding down the distinguished position of driver-batman. Now I can say I have done everything!"

*   *   *

Although Germany's surrender came more quickly than expected, and separately on various battlefields rather than in one major decision from the highest level, it did not catch the Allies unawares. For months they had been preparing for victory and for the occupation and demilitarization of Germany. Their plan, Operation Eclipse, was "designed to ensure that once and for all no possible shadow of doubt shall be left in the mind of a single German that the military might of the Third Reich has been shattered," says paragraph seven of Report No. 174 referred to above. This goal was to be achieved in both destructive — "to ensure that the military might of the Reich is rendered completely innocuous ... for all time" — and constructive ways — "to re-establish law and order so that ... a new German government can emerge and the re-education of the German national can take place."

The report says the government of Canada had approved the participation of Canadian troops in the British Army of Occupation in December 1944, and planning began immediately for the long-term Canadian occupation force created in June 1945. It was named 3rd Canadian Division, Canadian Army Occupation Force (CAOF), to distinguish it from the operational 3rd Division that had landed in Normandy on D-Day. Its three brigades were designated 2nd 7th, 2nd 8th and 2nd 9th (written 2/7, 2/8 and 2/9) to distinguish them from the original 3rd Division brigades that fought through the war. Many of the same regiments were involved; for example, the Regina Rifles, Royal Winnipeg Rifles and 1st Canadian Scottish of the 7th Brigade all formed new 4th battalions on June 1 for 2/7 Brigade of the CAOF. With ancillary troops, Canada would contribute a maximum of 25,000 men, all ranks, to the occupation of Germany.

A letter written on January 12, 1945 from Canadian Army Chief of Staff Lieutenant-General P.J. Montague to the Under Secretary of State in the War Office at Whitehall, in London, and included as an appendix to Report No. 174, explains how the men were to be chosen. They would either be volunteers "willing to forego *(sic)* their priority of demobilization" or officers and men with a low priority of demobilization who were assigned. Since a considerable number of Canadians were in their sixth year of service overseas, and many more had spent three years or more abroad, the government felt that Canadian forces should be repatriated "as quickly as circumstances will permit," General Montague said. Canada would not promise to keep troops in Europe for the entire period of military control in Germany, but would review the decision before March 31, 1946. Later, high level discussions about the future occupation made it "increasingly evident that the Canadian Government would have no voice in the direction of the policy for the control of Germany," says Report No. 174, paragraph 79. The Canadian Army Occupation Force began to leave Europe in May of 1946 and was disbanded in June. Probably no one in it was sorry.

Charles Reid of Dilke was one of those who volunteered for occupation duty. After serving in Italy and Europe with the British Columbia Dragoons of the 5th Armoured Division, he moved to the 17th Duke of York's Royal Canadian Hussars, 2/7 Reconnaissance Regiment, CAOF. His brief letters show that he received three parcels, two packages of cigarettes and one box of chocolates from the Comfort Club during his six months in Germany, a period he remembers very clearly. "That country was just beat down to nothing," he says. "They didn't have enough to eat. They didn't have enough of anything." He saw people scratching around in places where locomotive ashes had been dumped; they might find "one little piece of coal and they really thought they had something." He says the people he met "didn't all think the way Hitler did. The way I got it, the young ones were brainwashed but the older people, say the people in the generation older than me or even some my age, they didn't go along with it — they went along with it, they had to, but they didn't support him. They didn't like what he was doing. That's the impression I got. And then things were so bad there that I suppose they blamed him for it. I suppose in a way some of them blamed the Allies. When you stop to think of it, they brought it on themselves."

Reid figures he got back to Canada from his occupation duties just as quickly as if he had stayed with the B.C. Dragoons. "While I was in Germany, they were in England. They didn't get home ahead of me by very much." He arrived in July 1946.

Another Dilke veteran of the CAOF was Gunnar Gustafson, who had not been long in England before he went to Holland with 2/8 Infantry Brigade Workshop of the Royal Canadian Electrical and Mechanical Engineers. He wrote to the Comfort Club almost every month, long, informative letters about what he was seeing and doing. "At present we are getting organized in the south of Holland and expect to move into Germany this coming week," he wrote on July 1, 1945 from Amersfoot. "However I have high hopes that it won't be for any great length of time but we'll know more definitely after things are straightened around. At the present time, things are pretty well mixed up as they are doing a lot of shifting of troops." The Comfort Club's latest package of 300 Sweet Caporal cigarettes led to these observations by the father of two young daughters: "As the children over here in Holland say, 'smokie for poppa.' Another of their expressions is 'shock-o-lat for me or cow-kun (gum).' You never walk up the street without hearing their sayings a dozen times, a favourite excuse being someone's birthday tomorrow, some have a birthday every day. Tobacco is very scarce and picking cigarette butts is very common, in the early morning when we were on duty we even see some of the more modest ones out dooling up and down the streets getting their supply for the day. Chocolate, candy & gum are like gold and so in many cases are the root of a great deal of evil."

His next letter came from Aurich, 130 miles northeast on Germany's West Friesland peninsula. "So far I fail to see why the Jerry fought so hard, for in this part of the country they are far from as well off as any of the other places I have been. This is mostly a farming district and so everyone is busy putting up hay at present. Crops look good & we have been getting plenty of rain the past few days." As the official driver for his unit's Officers Mess, Gustafson went around the country dealing for food, meeting lots of people in the process. He was glad of the work, for otherwise "things would be very hard on morale for so far there is nothing for us to do." He found the farms very different from Canadian farms and much smaller. "They also still carry on the old tradition of living in colonies large enough to make a little village. Their shortages at present seem to be mostly meat, tea, coffee, sugar, soap & flour but believe that before winter is over they will find things very hard. People from the cities have all moved to the country so you find several families in most houses. So far we have run into no trouble here. The majority are starting to come down to earth and the harder things get, the sooner they will straighten out. Being able to talk to them now will educate them to what has been going on in other countries for they have really been led like the blind and are ignorant as to what has happened."

When he wrote on September 18, Gustafson was just back from a short leave in England. "We left Aurich by truck at 7 a.m. arriving in Oldenburg at 7 a.m.*[sic]* where we met the convoy. From there to Nymegen in Belgium. This took us until 5.30 that evening so you can see it is quite a truck ride. There we entered the transit camp for supper and caught the train at 6 o'clock for Calais. We were really packed in and all coaches had wooden seats. This trip took until 7 the next morning and by then I can truly say I was glad to get out as I was too sore to sit any longer. Inside of one hour we had breakfast, went though customs and were on the boat. It took 1½ hours to cross the channel. We docked at Dover so saw the White Cliffs of Dover." He saw friends in London and enjoyed being able to understand what people were saying, perhaps making the pain of travel worthwhile.

When he returned to his outfit, he found it had relocated north and east to an airport three miles from Jever, closer to the North Sea and about 15 miles from Wilhelmshaven. "They are using the hangars for the workshop and the billets all over the hangers. We also have some airforce and artillery here so they are still using the airport. Planes land & take off almost every day. The big trouble is there is not a thing here. We have one show a week in our mess hall. For other entertainment we have to go by truck to the larger points. There are no canteens or showers any closer than fifteen miles so you can see it isn't very handy. We have had our leaves cut to one leave every 4½ months now, so this isn't going to help pass the time very quickly. We were getting a 72 hour pass every month and a 12 day leave every three months, in this way a person always had a thing to look forward to. So hope they decide soon that they don't need us much longer so we can get home and live our own lives."

By October 15, the weather was cool, in Germany and in Dilke. "So it should be a good time to throw a few shovelfuls of coal on the stove and go to town only we are still minus the stove, and from all reports you are minus coal. But we aren't quite so badly off for we managed to scrounge a coal oil heater which is enough to take off the chill at present. Understand we are to get 4 lbs. of coal per person this winter so it looks like a cold winter. Guess we will have to go bushwhacking or else start in on the hangar. Things were warm here for a while today for the kitchen was on fire." He had driven the liberty truck to Wilhelmshaven the day before, he said. "I went all through the port in the truck and spent the whole afternoon looking at many different kinds of ships, had my camera along and got several shots of some of the large battleships, destroyers, sailboats etc. Also of the submarine base and a floating pier. All in all, it proved a very interesting afternoon." It might be surprising that he was trusted with the liberty truck for he had previously taken it to Oldenburg, a bigger city south of Wilhelmshaven, and did not bring it back. "I went to an early show and then returned to the truck to get my coat only to find it missing. To date nothing has been heard of it. Some soldier must have thought he needed it more than we did for it was in a military car park & only a soldier could have taken it out."

In a letter written on December 13 that is as revealing today as it would have been in 1945, Gustafson reported in detail on a lecture about the occupation given by the Military Governor of the British Zone. "Their first step is to get the Gov't working smoothly, then it will be gradually turned over to civilians here once they are drilled in the ways of democracy. The next is to get the economic set-up working. This is in the hands of experts from the U.S.A., England, Russia and France and the whole future of the world depends on how these plans work out. The number of displaced personnel in our zone is eight million and [the] problem of greatest concern is to find food, fuel and shelter for everyone. The civilians have been warned that they will receive no fuel this winter so have to scrounge wood and peat. The calorie rating is less than 1550 at the present time but they are trying to build it up to this level for winter. This I think will explain the food condition. This is one of the most destructed countries in history so you will understand the housing condition, it is far from good.

"Of those travelling into the zone daily many are passing on en route to their destination. Of the displaced personal they expect about four and a half million to perish during the winter. With these conditions facing us, you can see that a very strict control is going to have to be kept in effect in order to keep down the organizing of gangs that might cause considerable disorder. To give you an idea of how badly the population is displaced, about thirty-five percent of the children in the zone know the whereabouts of their parents, the rest are being taken care of as best they can. Whole families are at a loss as to the whereabouts of the rest and have had no contact for months. These conditions will not help much for it is bad enough having to be away when you know that they are getting along fairly well. We are located in the richest agricultural part of Germany so the cities are going to be the main source of trouble. At the present time they are just producing enough coal for our needs and the essential industries. Should we have much bad weather, we will be without power as the stocks are so low. This means that there will only be enough coal to keep us warm.

"The main sore spot now seems to be the Russians and so many of the rumors that are floating around are founded in this country in order to try and cause discontent between the allies and Russia. We were assured that this need not be a concern for that all was working in harmony and that the Russians were working to their utmost to make this a world of peace. They are having their share of trouble as the Germans used the scorched earth policy on their retreat and this has left some pretty hard conditions. The big reason for hating the Russian is the fact that the Russian is treating the German the same as he was treated and so fear is playing its part. If you have followed the trials you will understand why and especially so if you have seen any of the concentration films for they are things that will never be forgotten. But if things go according to latest write-ups, we will all be out of here in the spring and I'm sure there will be very few who will be sorry." This is the only reference to concentration camps in all the Dilke letters.

Gustafson was busy with a correspondence course, he wrote then, but in February he was disappointed that he was not allowed to play hockey. "As you have likely read, we are having hockey games etc. over here and you may think that we should have a pretty fair time. But so is not the case. It is alright for those that are playing, but for those of us that are not it is of no good for the games are all played outside of Germany and so we are unable to enjoy them. I tried to get away to play hockey but the 2I/C would not let me go. So all the hockey that we get is what we read in our own paper. This is the case with a great many things that we are supposed to be enjoying."

Perhaps for that reason he so much appreciated the letters and parcels from the Comfort Club, and especially the funny papers. "The boys really go for them as this is something that we are unable to get and it doesn't seem to matter how old one gets, they always seem to enjoy the funnies."

Gustafson did not mention seeing any other Dilke men while he was stationed in Aurich, but Fred Blancheon of the South Saskatchewan Regiment wrote to the Comfort Club from there on June 26. Everything looked quiet and peaceful, he reported. "The Germans are behaving themselves pretty good so far; they are really a badly beaten race of people." Looking toward the big celebration promised for Dominion Day, July 1, he rather wistfully remembered attending the annual sports day at Bethune, 14 miles from Dilke, on that day five years before. "In five more days it will be five years since I last saw Dilke," he said. "It sure has slipped by fast." He hoped to be out of the army by November, "all being well."

When Blancheon wrote next, on August 10, he was based in Amersfoort in Holland and had just returned from a leave in England to visit his wife, Mary. "I guess most of the boys will soon be home from over here. There's a lot to go yet, surprising how long it will take to get them all home." He would not be returning to Canada, but his farming experience told. "Well, folks, I guess you are at the harvest, hope you have a good crop, maybe we'll be needing some good flour for bread soon." On September 20, he wrote happily, "Today they are starting to move the 2nd Div from here to England on our second lap of the journey home." His section would leave on September 26, he said, "we have only 6 more days and they are really going slow." He hoped that he could get his demobilization in England, without having to return to Canada, and so it proved. When he wrote his final letter to the Comfort Club on November 20, he was still in a repatriation camp "but hope for my discharge soon as I intend to live here. I should have been out by now, but they lost all my papers and I had to go on leave to get more." The rest of the South Saskatchewan Regiment was back in Canada, but Blancheon never saw this country again.

Others began to get a little fed up, and a new expression entered their vocabulary: frozen. Ernest Burns wrote on July 22 from the 12th Canadian Light Field Ambulance of the Royal Canadian Army Medical Corps; he had been moved from the Signals Corps' 4th Armoured Brigade. "I have been transposted as you see, but expect to be here for some months yet as we are frozen or something. Some expect we will be here for Xmas this year. I rather think we will but one never knows. But we will be back and that's the main thing." Lloyd Carr, now with the Provost Corps, was less resigned. "I am one of the frozen few over here so will be here for some time yet," he wrote bitterly on July 3. "It seems they don't give a damn whether or not a long service man ever gets home or not. (He had enlisted in September 1940). I have enough points that I should have been home or on my way by now. I was willing to give my life in battle but I'll be damned if I care to die an old man over here. I am sure if the people back home would raise enough stink they could get us home much sooner. Our Government has really let us down. It's not only my opinion but that of many hundreds more who are frozen as I." He was still frozen in late September, when he wrote, "I may make it home before spring but it's hard to take, being a high point man and these Joes who were forced into the army are getting home. Some out of the army, too. It's tough medicine to take but God wishing it, I'll be home some day." On October 15, he advised the Comfort Club to send him no more cigarettes. "I am almost sure I will be leaving here some time next or the very first of the next month."

Carr finally reached home in February of 1946, travelling on the *Queen Elizabeth* to New York and then to Weyburn, Saskatchewan, where his wife Nellie was living and where they still live today. He remembers that soldiers like himself with long service had been urged to return home "and get rested and go over to the Japanese war." Instead, he and many others decided to stay where they were. "By doing so, after the war was over we were still held over. Like the war was over in '45 and we never come back until '46." People in the Provost Corps had to locate Canadians who were missing, living out, absent without leave, he says. "That was one of our jobs ... It disturbed a lot of people in their lives."

Still others had opted to stay on, almost to their own surprise. On August 17, Clarence Wray told the Comfort Club that many men had been re-posted to different regiments "so they will all be lined up to be ready to go home as Div (Division)." Some men were leaving the next day on repat drafts, he said, and he hoped to be on his way pretty soon. "It sort of makes your blood boil when you see chaps go home that haven't been in the army any more than three years." Like Carr, he had enlisted in 1940. But when he wrote to Helen and Ernie Mortin on November 4 from England, things had changed. "I came over here last month on my way home. I got a chance to stay here for a spell so I have volunteered for another six months in this country or until most of the troops will be out of the country." To these friends, he wrote: "Don't say it. I know what you're thinking. But I have a very good job. And at least I know what I will be doing until spring. And it will be much better to start in the spring than this time of year." It was a nice camp with cosy billets and nothing to worry about with the war over. "I'm in charge of four spiders here, and hope to get a promotion soon."

In January 1946, he wrote that they were "kept very busy trying to get the Canucks home ... Some days we get as high as two thousand men going out and maybe the same number coming in. I have been here since September, and at that time I signed on for six months. So that means it will be March before I will be leaving here. There are rumours now that they may keep this camp open for some time yet, and maybe they will use it for the CAOF. It is kind of hard on the nerves to see so many men going home. But I guess our turn will be coming; at least we still have a job to do here."

\*    \*    \*

Dilke men in the RCAF were just as keen to get home. Some, like bomber pilot Sam Side who had completed his first tour and been instructing, left England for Canada in January 1945, pending a second tour. He was returning to Western command in Winnipeg as the leave was ending but was posted instead to Gimli, Manitoba to fly with the

Winter Experimental and Testing Flight. He flew a Lancaster, testing different engines for cold weather flight, and was in Gimli when the war ended. He was discharged in Regina in October 1945.

Others in the RCAF, including aero-engine mechanics Albert Horne and Gus Koch from Dilke, signed up for the RAF's Tiger Force to serve in the Pacific. As originally planned, Tiger Force involved three very long range bomber groups — one from the Royal Air Force, one from the RCAF and one British Commonwealth formation with men from Britain, Australia, New Zealand and South Africa. By the spring of 1945 it had been scaled back to two groups, which were to begin training in August and reach the Pacific by December. The RCAF contribution was No. 6614 Wing Greenwood, with squadrons 405, 408, 419, 420, 425, 428, 431 and 434. Japan's surrender on August 14 made the whole plan superfluous.

Albert Horne of 434 Squadron came home on the *Ile de France*, once a big luxury liner. "All the luxury part was taken out," he remembers, "and they had hammocks all close together and about four or five hammocks one above the other, so the boat was really crowded. The messhall opened early in the morning and operated continuously throughout the day to way late at night, and people had to take turns in having their meals," which he thinks were limited to two per day. He took his disembarkation leave in Dilke and then, even though the war with Japan was over, had to go to Moncton, New Brunswick to get his discharge from Tiger Force, so he visited relatives in Prince Edward Island. Gus Koch of 420 Squadron arrived in Regina on leave on V-J Day, so he knew he wouldn't be going to the Pacific theatre. "Before we got off the train in Regina, they had already sent notices right across throughout the whole troop train: You must stay at the address you have designated so they could contact you. Although Japan had capitulated, they didn't know what other areas of combat were involved." He was home in Dilke for about a month before he was called into Regina for discharge.

Possibly the strangest experience of the war's end belongs to David Barss. As soon as he turned 17½, he left Dilke to join the army in Regina. He stayed with Bob Naldrett at his parents' home there, and the two teenagers decided to enlist together in the air force. Barss did so, but somehow Naldrett ended up joining the navy. After his basic air force training, Barss left Halifax for England — two days before V-E Day, May 8, 1945. They weren't permitted to leave the convoy and return to Canada. After landing in Liverpool, they moved to the south coast of England, where the RCAF bases were being closed down. "I was trained as a gunner but I never got off the ground when I got over there," he remembers. He spent half his time in Britain on leave, and was on his way to see an aunt in Scotland when he stopped in Glasgow and met Betty McRae. It was love at first sight. "I spent all my leaves in Scotland after that," he says, and they were soon married. He was discharged in April of 1946 and she followed him to Canada in June.

When they finally came home after their years overseas, some Dilke men brought more than their memories. Nine war brides crossed the ocean to join their husbands, sometimes with children in tow. Among them were Alan and Lil Wilton, top; Reece and Jean Jones, centre; and Jack and Roni Naldrett, bottom.

# Chapter X.

# THE "BOYS" COME HOME

IN dribs and drabs, the men from Dilke reached home to a joyous welcome that began almost as soon as their ships landed. Sam Side remembers that wherever his train stopped between Halifax and Regina, it was met by groups and organizations offering gifts of goodies and warm appreciation. "And then when we got home," he recalls, "there was a whole platform of friends." Steve Eberts sailed to New York on the *Queen Elizabeth* and then west by troop train to Regina, where "most of my family was there to meet us." Hundreds of people crowded the armories where they met their families, he says. Charles Ell's mother met him at the station. "She sat down and cried."

Ell is still amazed at the things he noticed when he first got home. He landed in Halifax on New Year's Day in 1946, "and as we were marching from the ship to the train, we'd pass some stores and windows and we marvelled at the amount of goods that were in the shop windows. Soap, which I'd never thought I'd ever notice. Because we were issued a ration of soap during the time we were in England, we came to appreciate soap. And oranges and apples, things like that we take for granted now. And the amount of different things that you saw in shops ... that weren't available in England."

Dilke celebrated the return of its long-lost children. "They usually had a big get-together in the hall for everybody that came back, a welcome home," Charles Reid says. "Sometimes there would be two or three at once, it depends on when they came back." Joe Ell remembers such a party. "I made a big speech, I can't remember what, must have been a bunch of baloney." Albert Horne somehow missed out on the welcoming parties at the station in Regina and in Dilke. But he has a telling answer when he's asked if it felt strange to be back in peaceful Canada. "It's just something you take for granted, that it's going to be peaceful."

What seemed strangest to Joe Ell after his years in Britain was the flatness of Saskatchewan and the lack of trees. But the hometown? "It seemed it was still Dilke."

*     *     *

And though Dilke was the place they had dreamed of through their years away, for some of them it soon became part of their problem. Like all veterans, they returned to Canada with their vistas widened by experiences not shared — and perhaps not even imaginable — by the folks who had lived through the war safe at home. For many, settling back into their pre-war world of farm or village was not possible. As the song says, "How do you keep them down on the farm, after they've seen Paree?" Nonetheless, 14 of those who went from Dilke — Lester Duesing, Regina Eberts (the only woman from the district who served overseas, in the RCAF Women's Division), Steve Eberts, Charles Ell, Albert Horne, Reece Jones, Charles Reid, Leo Selinger, Mike Selinger, Lawrence Smith, Lloyd Smith, Bert Tait, George Tait and Clarence Wray — did return to farming as a career, in the Dilke area or elsewhere in Saskatchewan. Some took over the family farm, others eventually achieved their own farm, and they lived and worked there, raising their families, until they retired. If they ever longed for foreign fields, they kept it hidden.

Charles Ell remembers how different the farm seemed when he reached Dilke in 1946. He had last been there in June 1942, on embarkation leave before he went overseas, "and Dad and I went out to the fields and the crops were withering and it was dry." It seemed like the 1930s all over again. "In August, when they wrote and told me what a good crop there was, I couldn't believe it. It must have started raining in June and July." By today's yield standards of 35-40 or more bushels to the acre, it wasn't that great, he says, just 20 bushels, "but compared to nothing 20 was good for the Dilke area." While he was away, his father had enlarged and rebuilt the house, so things were different. Part of that difference was due to Ell and his brother Joe. "Of course the fact that we were sending half our money — overseas we were only allowed a dollar a day and the rest went to our parents at home. All of a sudden they had this ready cash. And the fact, too, that the crops had improved so much." In 1946, he was working for Macleod's in Winnipeg when he married Bernadette Wolfe, with whom he had corresponded throughout the war, and they moved to Regina. But in 1948, when they had a chance to take over her mother's farm at Liberty, they jumped at it, and farmed until 1987, when they were succeeded by their son. Ell continues to play in a dance band, just as he did during the war. What he learned because he played the saxophone is the most lasting influence of his years in the army.

Even back on the farm, Steve Eberts found that the sound of airplanes scared him. It took about a year to get over shrinking from that, he remembers, or his response to the sight of blood. "People didn't know what we went through. I don't even like talking about it, unless I'm asked or it's someone who's been there." He farmed south of Dilke for a few years and then moved to a farm near Lumsden, 24 miles away, where he stayed until he retired. "We did what we had to do," he says with finality about his war service. "Can't say I felt like a hero."

Other Dilke men, too, returned to the careers they had abandoned when they answered their country's call. Joe Ell, Frank Selinger and Jim Wilton went back to teaching, though Ell attended university immediately after the war. Tuition was free but they bought their own books, he remembers, and were paid $60 a month during the seven months of study. Since he had been to Normal School before the war, he earned an education degree in three years. "Then, when Russia put up the first Sputnik, ahead of the Americans, and we said we have to give our kids tougher math and science and there were new math, physics, chem and biology books, I took a year off and went back to university to get my arts degree." He stayed in Saskatchewan, but Jim Wilton did his postwar teaching in Alberta communities, and retired to British Columbia.

Unlike many of the Dilke veterans, Ell remains in contact with the men of his crew in Royal Air Force 15 Squadron. He and his wife Velma took in a squadron reunion in London in 1981, which was also attended by Sir Arthur Harris, the head of Bomber Command, aged 89. "We were the only crew there intact, so we had our picture taken with him." Ell sighs a little, looking at the photograph. "I stood straight and tall in those days," he says. "I loved to be straight." Severe osteoporosis of the lower spine has changed that.

In the same way, Lloyd Smith attended reunions in British Columbia of the 14th Canadian Hussars (8th Recce Regiment) but has had to give them up because he no longer drives. His arm wound did not trouble him or stop him from driving a car or a tractor when he was farming, though. Except for his time in the army, and since his retirement, farming has been his life. He says he didn't worry about getting out of the army until seeding started in the spring of 1945. He helped his brother put in a crop that year.

While still in Europe with the Occupation Force, Gunnar Gustafson had begun to worry about finding a job when he did get home. Unlike many of his fellows from Dilke, he had a wife and two daughters to support. "We know that the people who have taken over jobs that had to be given up due to the war feel that the release has been too fast and that it has caused a great deal of unemployment, and with the servicemen out of work there has come some cause for anxiety," he wrote home in February 1946. He didn't feel that the men still in Europe should be the goat for this, however. "After all, we have our families and loved ones that also need us as much as we need them, and if the Government feel that they have to do occupational duty, they should arrange it so that not only a few suffer but that it be spread out so no one has to do any great length of time." He became an elevator agent in Dilke after he returned, and he and his wife Margaret also ran the post office. Later, he became manager of the Dilke Co-op, and then moved around Western Canada with the Co-Op system.

*     *     *

For many others from Dilke, life was completely changed after the war, and they spread across Canada in a wide range of occupations, from carpentry to meat-cutting, from forestry to gardening. Two navy veterans, Bob Naldrett and Walter Wilton, joined the RCAF.

Gus Koch had joined up at 22 after doing a mechanics course through the Dominion-Provincial Youth Training School; he was taking a correspondence course in diesel mechanics from National Schools of Los Angeles when he enlisted. Now it was late 1945. He had been gone more than four years, doing a job he knew was important in the most important thing in the world at the time, and now the adventure was over. "You more or less stood with your hands in your pocket and said, 'What do I do now?'" He had a new wife to provide for, and he did not think he could do that in his hometown. "I think through the latter part of my service I realized there was nothing in Dilke that would support our lifestyle and we would definitely have to move on," he says now. He and his Spitfire pilot brother Tom decided to go into a business, and after flirting with the idea of a grocery store, they bought a garage at Middle Lake, Saskatchewan in 1946. The next year he left and went to work with the provincial Highways Department as a mechanic, based in Regina. "It was quite different from bombers, yes, but mechanical training — once you get the basics of it — fits in pretty well all over."

It wasn't quite as exciting as servicing aircraft, he admits with a laugh. "You didn't have the feeling that life and death was dependent on you." But what he had learned served him in good stead. "One of the things that was really impressed on you was, hey, boys, it better be right. And I think that in itself stayed with me the rest of my life. I had to be a perfectionist." He rose to become equipment manager for the department in Regina, and he and Heather made their home there. Tom Koch ended up with the Department of National Revenue, where he worked for more than 17 years, until his retirement in 1980.

While Butch and Sam Side were overseas, their family had left Dilke for Edmonton and opened a restaurant there. Both brothers went to work in the restaurant when they got home, doing eight-hour shifts. "It took two years to recover," Sam Side says. "We were pretty wild kids" — so wild that after one of their escapades in England, Butch was demoted from corporal to lance-corporal for not getting back to barracks on time. "Sam never knew that but for that 10 cents, I had to not cry too loud," he says now. But they had a pretty good time when they were living in Edmonton, too.

Looking back, Sam Side reflects that the war took five years of their lives, which may be why they took two years to recover. "The thing that straightened us out more was getting married and kids started to come along." He married Ann Kucharak in 1949. "There comes a time when you have to take life seriously. Having children brings responsibilities." Instead of going back to university, Side started a bush pilot business in northern British Columbia and Alberta from Dawson Creek, B.C. in 1947. He also operated a flying school. The war changed the entire pattern of his life, he says. "I wouldn't know where my life would have ended up, what would have happened if it hadn't been for ... the thing was, we gained an awful lot of knowledge about life and the world and travel the way we did. In the circumstances, that had its very beneficial effect on us. But there was the other side, in that we became totally irresponsible."

His brother Butch also found himself on a new path because of what he had learned in the war. His office experience led to similar kinds of work in Alberta. He met his wife Marie in Edmonton and then got a job in the office of a coal company in Lescar, Alberta. "I went to the coal mine, black as black as black could be, wearing white shirts and all dressed up with a tie and everything else, and they say, he's not going to stay." He stayed for more than three years. Later, he moved into the oilfield business, as a company's chief estimator and sales co-ordinator, "and you had to have purchasing, you had to learn everything ... there's only one sales co-ordinator, so if there's any problem you're the problem." He believes that his army experience helped in later life. "It made me smart enough — we worked for nothing or next to nothing, we begged, borrowed, stole whatever you could get." Such experience "made life better for you and your family, I mean in the long run."

Some of his experiences overseas did anything but make life better for Lloyd Carr. He was shell-shocked in Italy and the effects stayed with him, requiring shock treatments in a psychiatric centre in Weyburn. He joined the police force in Moose Jaw when he first returned to Canada, but could find no home there for his wife Nellie and their two children. After several different jobs in Weyburn, he became caretaker for the provincial courthouse there in 1949 and stayed until retirement in 1982. He took up again the saxophone he had to leave behind when he shipped off for Italy and is still part of a band that plays for dances and entertains seniors' organizations and in nursing homes.

*    *    *

None of the Dilke men suggest that they regret in any way the sizable pieces of their lives they gave to Canada's war against the Axis powers. They would probably all agree with Joe Ell that it was a great experience. They just hope it will never be required of another generation of Canadians. And they aren't sure it won't.

When he was interviewed in August 2000, 58 years to the day after he sailed from Halifax to England, Charles Ell recalled a television program on which people in their 30s were interviewed about the war. "They didn't seem to think that the war was worthwhile, that we could have used some other means of stopping Hitler. I don't know what they would mean by that. I can't think of any other means, but they seemed to think that maybe we didn't use the right approach. Now this was just one group of people, but it is depressing to think that maybe we had spent a lot of our time ... we lost a lot of boys too, a lot of young men."

"We don't seem to have accomplished anything," Charles Reid feels. "I mean it's going to turmoil again." But the war was necessary "because if we wouldn't have done anything, they would have overrun the whole world." He and the other Dilke men did not come home hating the Germans they had fought, but they did hate the man those Germans followed, Adolf Hitler. As Lloyd Smith put it, "Why a maniac like that could get that strong, he went through all them countries just a-going." Still, he thinks the world has changed for the better.

Lloyd Carr would do it again. "If I was that age again, knowing what I know now, I'd certainly do it." He is somewhat bitter, though, that the efforts made by so many Canadians for so long in Italy are not more appreciated here. He lives in Weyburn, the home of the South Saskatchewan Regiment that suffered so badly at Dieppe, and so he hears a lot about the raid on occasions when the war is remembered.

"What they fail to remember, what they fail to announce, is because of our endeavours in Italy ... we had some of the toughest German and Italian soldiers that were available during the war. Because we were making so much progress and pounding them so hard, it kept their forces from being available in France" for D-Day. "In our opinion, [D-Day] would never have gone on as it did had it not been for the terrific action we were applying through Italy ... They would have had to sacrifice an awful lot more than what they did." The best German units, armour and infantry, were being held in Italy because of the under-appreciated struggles, through mud and mountains, of men some called the D-Day dodgers and who proudly, contemptuously, adopted the name as their own.

*     *     *

As the years passed, the Dilke people who returned from overseas put the war behind them, packed their memories away and got on with earning a living and raising a family. They forgot about the Comfort Club that connected them with home throughout their years overseas, though when they were asked about it for this book, they had fond memories of the parcels, cigarettes, chocolates, letters and love that kept coming from Dilke. Their final letters from Europe are filled with gratitude and praise for the women who packed the parcels and the community that sacrificed to provide them. "Thanks for all the parcels and cigarettes you have sent me since I have been overseas," Charles Reid summed up in the last letter in the Comfort Club files, written on May 5, 1946 from Germany though he expected to be home by summer.

And that's the story of the little prairie town that gave 101 of its children to Canada's war, of the 62 of those children who went overseas and bravely did their part, and of the Comfort Club that truly sent them comfort wherever they went during those grim years. It's half a century and more since they wrought their ploughshares into swords and guns and went off to foreign lands to fight for freedom and democracy, for their country and their little hometown. They came home and took up their lives again, although seven did not come home, and they were not forgotten in that hometown. Few of the people who feature in this book call Dilke home today, nor, if they visited, would they recognize the town they knew without its elevators, its railroad, its school. Many are dead now, and maybe we didn't tell them often enough, but to those of us who benefit still from their sacrifices, they are all heroes.

Quiet, unassuming heroes from a quiet little prairie town — Dilke, Saskatchewan.

# THANKS AND ACKNOWLEDGMENTS

Many people have contributed in many ways to the creation of this book. I am grateful for their support of my effort to tell the story of the men and women from my little hometown who served overseas during the Second World War and of the Comfort Club that supported them so staunchly.

I could have done nothing without the generous help and co-operation of the Dilke veterans, the families of those veterans who have died since the war and the families of the seven men who were killed. They have permitted me to quote from letters to the Comfort Club, they have dug through trunks and boxes to locate photographs and they have encouraged me with their interest and enthusiasm. I thank them most sincerely, and only wish the book had been completed sooner, when more of the Dilke veterans were still living.

From the day I found the Comfort Club letters, my family has supported me in this project. The tie with the past through my parents, Helen and Ernie Mortin, who were part of the Club, was invaluable. My sisters Linda Ferguson and Sharon Jeeves were always supportive, and my brother David Mortin scanned many photos. Members of my extended family were also helpful and encouraging, as were friends across Canada. I thank them all, especially those who read the manuscript and offered helpful advice.

In Saskatoon, Michael Gillgannon scanned dozens of old photos and Brian Johnsrude created the indispensable maps. Thank you both. And thanks to George Vanderburgh, whose publishing courage and know-how made it possible to tell the story you have read.

— Jenni Mortin

# Appendix I
# Men and Women from Dilke and District Who Joined Canada's Armed Forces in the Second World War.

| | | | |
|---|---|---|---|
| Amberson, Dave | Navy | Lipp, Michael | Army |
| Amberson, Dean | Army | MacKay, Ted | Army *then* RCAF |
| Anderson, Clarence | RCAF | Madson, Svend | Army |
| Anderson, Otto | RCAF | Mangel, John | Army |
| Barry, Ernest | Army | Massine, Anthony | Army |
| Barry, John | Army | McEwen, Ivan | Army |
| Barry, Whitney | Army | McLeod, Allan | RCAF |
| Barss, David | RCAF | Naldrett, Jack | RCAF |
| Barss, Ellis | RCAF | Naldrett, John | Veterans Guard |
| Baukovy, Anne | CWAC | Naldrett, Bob V. | Navy |
| Blancheon, Fred | Army | Naldrett, Bob W. | Army |
| Boehme, Arthur | RCAF | Nugent, Frank | US Army |
| Boehme, Frank | Army | Rauch, Edythe | RCAF (WD) |
| Brandon, Edward | Army | Reid, Charles | Army |
| Buck, Harold | Army | Reid, John | RCAF **killed** |
| Buck, Leonard | RCAF | Schultz, Ted | Army |
| Burns, Ernest | Army | Scott, Walter | Army Medical Corps |
| Carr, Lloyd | Army | Selinger, Albert | Army |
| Church, Mayson | RCAF **killed** | Selinger, Frank | Army |
| Clark, Leslie | Army | Selinger, Leo | Army |
| Darby, Glen | Army | Selinger, Menrad | Army Medical Corps |
| Duesing, Lester | Army | Selinger, Mike | Army Medical Corps |
| Dunajski, Felix | Army | Selinger, Roy | Army |
| Dunajski, Francis | RCAF **killed** | Selinger, Tom | Army |
| Dunajski, Irwin | RCAF | Side, Abdul (Butch) | Army |
| Eberts, Regina | RCAF (WD) | Side, Netty | CWAC |
| Eberts, Steve | Army | Side, Sam | RCAF |
| Ell, Charles | Army | Silverthorn, Allan | RCAF **killed** |
| Ell, Joseph DFC | RCAF | Smith, Lawrence | Army |
| Farrow, Kenneth | Army | Smith, Lloyd | Army |
| Fuchs, Alex | RCAF | Steif, George | RCAF |
| Fuchs, Frank | Army **killed** | Tait, Alex | Army |
| Fuchs, Tony | Navy | Tait, Bert | Army |
| Gartner, Jerome | Army | Tait, Ethel | RCAF (WD) |
| Gartner, Eugene | Army | Tait, Francis | RCAF **killed** |
| Gerris, Edward | Army | Tait, George | RCAF |
| Gerris, George | Army | Tait, Robert | RCAF |
| Gustafson, Gunnar | Army | Tait, Walter | RCAF |
| Gwilym, Mary | RCAF (WD) | Tate, Dorothy | RCAF (WD) |
| Hein, John | Army | Tate, Joan | RCAF (WD) |
| Hills, Oliver | RCAF **killed** | Tate, John | Veterans Guard |
| Hoffart, John | Army | Tate, Walter | Army |
| Horne, Albert | RCAF | Thauberger, John | Army |
| Jones, Reece | RCAF | Thauberger, Peter | Army |
| Klein, Edward | RCAF | Wettstein, Ralph | Army |
| Klein, John | Army | Wilton, Lenore | RCAF (WD) |
| Koch, Frank | RCAF | Wilton, Alan | Army |
| Koch, Gus | RCAF | Wilton, Walter | Navy |
| Koch, Tom | RCAF | Wilton, James | Army |
| Laing, Stuart | Army | Wray, Clarence | Army |
| Laing, Doug | RCAF | | |

# Appendix II
# Men and Women of Dilke
# Who Served Overseas

| | | | |
|---|---|---|---|
| Amberson, Dean | Army | Koch, Tom | RCAF |
| Amberson, Dave | Navy | Laing, Stuart | Army |
| Barry, Ernest | Army | MacKay, Ted | RCAF |
| Barry, Whitney | Army | Mangel, John | Army |
| Barss, David | RCAF | Massine, Tony | Army |
| Blancheon, Fred | Army | McEwen, Ivan | Army |
| Boehme, Arthur | RCAF | Naldrett, Jack | RCAF |
| Boehme, Frank | Army | Naldrett, Bob W. | Army |
| Brandon, Edward | Army | Naldrett, Bob V. | Navy |
| Buck, Harold | Army | Reid, John | RCAF |
| Burns, Ernest | Army | | *Killed April 18, 1943* |
| Carr, Lloyd | Army | Reid, Charles | Army |
| Church, Mayson | RCAF | Schultz, Ted | Army |
| | *Killed July 30, 1943* | Scott, Walter | Army (Medical) |
| Duesing, Lester | Army | Selinger, Frank | Army |
| Dunajski, Francis | RCAF | Selinger, Leo | Army |
| | *Killed October 13, 1942* | Selinger, Mike | Army (Medical) |
| Eberts, Regina | RCAF (WD) | Side, Butch | Army |
| Eberts, Steve | Army | Side, Sam | RCAF |
| Ell, Charles | Army | Silverthorn, Allan | RCAF |
| Ell, Joe DFC | RCAF | | *Killed June 19, 1945* |
| Fuchs, Alex | RCAF | Smith, Lawrence | Army |
| Fuchs, Frank | Army | Smith, Lloyd | Army |
| | *Killed June 9, 1944* | Tait, Bert | Army |
| Fuchs, Tony | Navy | Tait, Francis | RCAF |
| Gartner, Jerome | Army | | *Killed January 28, 1942* |
| Gerris, Ed | Army | Tait, George | RCAF |
| Gustafson, Gunnar | Army | Tate, Jack | Army |
| Hills, Oliver | RCAF | Tate, Walter | Army |
| | *Killed June 23, 1943* | Thauberger, Pete | Army |
| Horne, Albert | RCAF | Wilton, Alan | Army |
| Jones, Reece | RCAF | Wilton, Jim | Army |
| Klein, John | Army | Wilton, Walter | Navy |
| Koch, Frank | RCAF | Wray, Clarence | Army |
| Koch, Gus | RCAF | | |

Dean Amberson

Ernest Barry

Whitney Barry

David Barss

Fred Blancheon

Arthur Boehme

Frank Boehme

Edward Brandon

Harold Buck

Ernest Burns

Lloyd Carr

Mayson Church
*Killed July 30, 1943*

Lester Duesing

Francis Dunajski
*Killed October 13, 1942*

Regina Eberts

Steve Eberts

Charles Ell

Joe Ell, DFC

Alex Fuchs

Frank Fuchs
*Killed June 9, 1944*

Tony Fuchs

Jerome Gartner

Ed Gerris

Gunnar Gustafson

Oliver Hills
*Killed June 23, 1943*

Albert Horne

Reece Jones

John Klein

Frank Koch

Gus Koch

Tom Koch

Stuart Laing

John Mangel

Ted MacKay

Ivan McEwen

Tony Massine

Jack Naldrett

Bob W. Naldrett

Bob V. Naldrett

John Reid
*Killed April 18, 1943*

Charles Reid

Ted Schultz

Walter Scott

Frank Selinger

Leo Selinger

Mike Selinger

Butch Side

Sam Side

Allan Silverthorn
*Killed June 19, 1945*

Lawrence Smith

Lloyd Smith

Bert Tait

Francis Tait
*Killed January 28, 1942*

George Tait

Jack Tate

Walter Tate

Pete Thauberger

Alan Wilton

Jim Wilton

Clarence Wray

No photos are available for
Dave Amberson (Navy)
and Walter Wilton (Navy).

# SOURCES

Minutes, accounts and address lists of the Dilke Active Service Comfort Club, 1940-45
Dilke column, *Craik Weekly News*, 1940-1945, Saskatchewan Archives, Regina, Saskatchewan
Dilke history book, *Ploughshares and Prairie Trails*
Letters to the Dilke Active Service Comfort Club, from:

Barry, Whitney, 1st Armoured Car Regiment (Royal Canadian Dragoons)

Barss, Dave, RCAF air gunner

Blancheon, Fred, South Saskatchewan Regiment

Boehme, Art, 419 Squadron, RCAF

Buck, Harold, 11th Army Field Regiment, Royal Canadian Artillery

Burns, Ernest, 4th Armoured Brigade, Royal Canadian Armoured Service Corps *then* 12th Light Field Ambulance, Royal Canadian Army Medical Corps

Carr, Lloyd, 2nd Armoured Regiment, (Lord Strathcona's Horse (Royal Canadians)) *then* Canadian Provost Corps

Eberts, Steve, 4th Reconnaissance Regiment (Princess Louise Dragoon Guards)

Ell, Charles, Royal Canadian Ordnance Corps

Ell, Joe, 15 Squadron, RCAF

Gartner, Jerome, Royal Canadian Ordnance Corps *then* 1st Canadian Scottish Regiment *then* No. 2 Base Reinforcement Group

Gustafson, Gunnar, #1 Canadian Signals Reinforcement Unit *then* 2/8 Infantry Brigade Workshop, Canadian Army Occupation Force

Horne, Albert, 434 Squadron, RCAF

Jones, Reece, 431 Squadron, RCAF

Koch, Frank, 415 Squadron, RCAF

Koch, Gus, 420 Squadron, RCAF

Koch, Tom, 401 Squadron, RCAF

Laing, Stuart, 13th Field Regiment, Royal Canadian Artillery *then* 17th Field Regiment

Mangel, Jack, 27th Armoured Regiment (Sherbrooke Fusiliers)

Naldrett, Bob, 8th Reconnaissance Regiment (14th Canadian Hussars)

Reid, Charles, 9th Armoured Regiment (British Columbia Dragoons)

Schultz, Ted, 14th Field Company, Royal Canadian Engineers

Selinger, Frank, Army

Selinger, Leo, Queen's Own Cameron Highlanders of Canada

Selinger, Mike, #5 Casualty Clearing Station, Royal Canadian Army Medical Corps

Side, Butch, No. 1, Canadian Armoured Corps Reinforcement Unit

Side, Sam, 428 Squadron, RCAF

Smith, Lloyd, 8th Reconnaissance Regiment (14th Canadian Hussars)

Tait, Bert, 8th Reconnaissance Regiment (14th Canadian Hussars)

Tate, Walter, 2nd Anti-Tank Regiment, Royal Canadian Artillery *then* 666 Squadron, RCAF

Thauberger, Pete, 3rd Field Survey Company, Royal Canadian Engineers

Wilton, Alan, 2nd Anti-Tank Regiment, Royal Canadian Artillery

Wray, Clarence, 2nd Canadian Light Anti-Aircraft Regiment

Personal interviews

Lloyd Carr, Weyburn, Saskatchewan, August 15, 2000

Steve Eberts, Lasalles Beach, Saskatchewan, September 9, 2000

Charles Ell, Liberty, Saskatchewan, August 10, 2000

Joe Ell, Shellbrook, Saskatchewan, July 7, 2000

Tony Fuchs, Regina, Saskatchewan, May 25, 2003

Albert Horne, Dilke, Saskatchewan, October 26, 2000

Gus Koch, Regina, Saskatchewan, June 1, 2000
Bob Naldrett, Regina, Saskatchewan, May 25, 2003
Charles Reid, Regina, Saskatchewan, June 2, 2000
Butch Side, Alberta Beach, Alberta, July 17, 2000
Sam Side, Dawson Creek, British Columba, July 18, 2000
Lloyd Smith, Regina, Saskatchewan, August 16, 2000

Telephone Interviews
Dave Barss, London, Ontario, 2003
Lester Duesing, Regina, Saskatchewan, 2003

# BIBLIOGRAPHY

*The major challenge in writing this book was to fix the Dilke people and their letters from the various arenas of war within the historical events as they occurred. It could not have been done without the books and websites I was able to consult. Particularly useful and valuable were those below marked with an asterisk.*

Allison, Les. *They Shall Grow Not Old: A Book of Remembrance*. Brandon, Man.: Commonwealth Air Training Plan Museum Inc., 1992.

Archer, John H. *Saskatchewan: A History*. Saskatoon: Western Producer Prairie Books, 1980.

Bracken, Robert. *Spitfire: The Canadians*. Erin, Ont.: Boston Mills Press, 1995.

Bracken, Robert. *Spitfire II: The Canadians*. Erin, Ont.: Boston Mills Press, 1999.

Buchanan, Lt. Col. G.B. *The March of the Prairie Men: A Story of the South Saskatchewan Regiment*. South Saskatchewan Regiment Regimental Association: Weyburn, Saskatchewan.

*Chandler, David G. and Collins, James Lawton Jr., eds. *The D-Day Encyclopedia*. New York: Simon & Schuster, 1994.

*Dancocks, Daniel G. *The D-Day Dodgers: The Canadians in Italy, 1943-1945*. Toronto: McClelland and Stewart Ltd., 1991.

Gossage, Carolyn. *Greatcoats and Glamour Boots: Canadian Women at War, 1939-1945*. Toronto: Dundurn Group, 2001.

Jackson, W.G.F. *The Battle for Rome*. London: B.T. Batsford Ltd., 1969.

*Leasor, James. *Green Beach*. London: Heineman Ltd., 1975.

Macpherson, Ken. *Frigates of the Royal Canadian Navy, 1943-1974*. St. Catharines, Ont.: Vanwell Publishing Ltd., 1989.

*McAndrew, Bill, Rawling, Bill and Whitby, Michael. *Liberation: The Canadians in Europe*. Montreal: Editions Art Global Inc., 1995.

Neillands, Robin and de Norman, Roderick. *D-Day, 1941: Voices from Normandy*. London: Weidenfeld and Nicolson, 1993.

Oglesby, Major R.B. "Canadian Organization in Theatres of Operation, 1939-1945". Report #53, Historical Section (GS), Army Headquarters, 11 June 1952, written for Col. C.P. Stacy, Director, Canadian Army Historical Section. www.dnd.ca/hr/dhh/Downloads/ahq/ahq053.PDF

*Ploughshares and Prairie Trails: Dilke & District*. Dilke, Saskatchewan: Dilke and District Historical Committee, 1982.

*Reader's Digest. *The Canadians at War, 1939/45*. 2nd ed. Editor, A.R. Byers. Westmount, Québec." The Reader's Digest Association (Canada) Ltd., 1986.

*Schull, Joseph. *Far Distant Ships: An Official Account of Canadian Naval Operations in World War II*. Toronto: Stoddart, 1987.

Shellor, John. *Forgotten Heroes: The Canadians at Dieppe*. Agincourt, Ont.: Methuen, 1975.

VIII Cdn Recce Regt 14CH. Battle History of the Regiment. 34-page booklet, undated.

*Whitaker, Brigadier-General Denis, Whitaker, Sheila and Copp, Terry. *Victory at Falaise: The Soldiers' Story*. Toronto: HarperCollins, 2000.

*Williams, Jeffery. *The Long Left Flank: The Hard Fought Way to the Reich, 1944-45*. Toronto: Stoddart, 1988.

Wilmot, Chester. *The Struggle for Europe*. London: Collins, 1965.

Zuehlke, Mark. *The Canadian Military Atlas: The Nation's Battlefields from the French and Indian Wars to Kosovo*. Text by Mark Zuehlke. Maps by C. Stuart Daniel. Toronto: Stoddart, 2001.

*Zuehlke, Mark. *Ortona: Canada's Epic World War II Battle*. Toronto: Stoddart, 1999.

# Websites

*www.vac-acg.gc.ca/general/sub.cfm?source=history/secondwar
www.vac-acc.gc.ca/general/sub
www.vac-acg.gc.ca/historical/secondwar/vrww2.htm
www.dnd.ca/hr/dhh/Downloads/cmhq/CMHQ174.PDF
www.cmcc.mus.digital.ca/cwm/cwmeng/cwmeng.htm
users.pandora.be/dave.depickere/Text/dieppe.html
www.legionmagaz9ine.com/features/canadianmilitaryhistory/01-11.asp
www.rcaca.org/r-LdSH.htm *also* RCD.htm; BCD.htm; GGHG.htm; 14H.htm; Sherbrooke.htm
www.islandnet.com/~csrmuse/
www.regiments.org/milhist/na-canada/volmil-man/inf/079QOCH.htm
www.regiments.org/milhist/na-canada/volmil-man/inf/090RWinR.htm
www.warchronicle/com/canadian_third_div/regimentals_wwii/pegs_dday.htm
www.regiments.org/milhist/na-canada/volmil-sask/inf/095Regina.htm
www.regiments.org/milhist/na-canada/volmil-sask/inf/920SSask.htm
cap.estevan.sk.ca/ssr/
www.regiments.org/milhist/na-canada/volmil-bc.inf/920caSco.htm
www.regiments.org/milhist/na-canada/corps.RCASC.htm
www.regiments.org/milhist/na-canada/corps.RCAMC.htm
www.multipointproductions.com/heroes/misc/orderbat/htm
pages.cthome.net/dryan/orders.canuk42.html
www.headley1.demon.co.uk/cdnoob.htm
dragon.acadiau.ca/~mike/army/inf/regt.html
www.navalmuseum.ab.ca/david.html
www.navy.dnd.ca/pride_html/history/ships_39_45/ships_39_45a4_c.htm
www.civilization.ca/orch/www04i_e.html
www.airforce.ca/wwii
www.airforce.forces.ca/14wing/about_ushistory7_e.asp
www.airforce.forces.ca/hist/ww_2_e.htm
www.lemuseum.org/ler/mh/wwii/airforce.html
collections.ic.gc.ca/books/texteng/rember.htm
org/tech/corsair.htm
www.tne.net.au/njh/Airpower/l(...
shearwateraviationmuseum.ns.ca/aircraft/specs/avrolancaster.htm
www.rcaf.com/squadrons/401sqn.shtml *also* 415sqn.shtml; 419sqn.shtml; 420sqn.shtml;
    428sqn.shtml; 429sqn.shtml; 431sqn.shtml; 166sqn.shtml;434sqn.shtml, 10sqn.shtml;
www.rcaf.com/squadrons/wwii_overseas.htm
www.raf.mod.uk/bombercommand/squadrons/h214.html *also* h156.html
www.aaca.org.uk/aop.htm428sqn.shtml
www.airforce.forces.ca/14wing/about_us/history7_e.asp

# INDEX

They were hardly more than kids when they left their little Saskatchewan town to enlist in Canada's war against fascism, fighting for democracy. Nearly one-fifth of the population of Dilke and its farming district enlisted during the Second World War, 101 in all, and 62 of those went overseas. Wherever the demands of war sent them – Britain, North Africa, Italy, Northwest Europe – the loving hand of home sustained them through letters and parcels, cookies and cigarettes from the Dilke Active Service Comfort Club. They responded with grateful letters filled with the story of their new lives in distant lands. Based on those letters, supplemented by the memories of the surviving veterans, *A Prairie Town Goes to War* celebrates the contribution made by Dilke people at home and abroad to Canada's tremendous war effort.

Born and raised in Dilke, Saskatchewan, Jenni Mortin left home to become a journalist. She has worked on four Canadian newspapers and taught journalism overseas, and is currently a freelance writer and editor located in Saskatoon. *A Prairie Town Goes to War* is her third book of Saskatchewan history.

"This is a gem of a book, local history at its finest."
— John Robert Colombo, author and anthologist